A
HAUNTING
PLACE

A HAUNTING PLACE

Bizarre, eerie and mysterious...
the world's most haunted places

GLEN WILLIAMS

NEW
HOLLAND

Contents

INTRODUCTION

We have all wandered in and out of haunted places. They're impossible to avoid. For the world is indeed a haunted place.

Most of us dismiss the idea of ghosts and hauntings as something kids love to talk about to give each other a playful scare.

Many of us like to wander through life, blissfully unaware, happily ignorant that we really are sharing this planet with a very spiritual world.

You only have to hear the number of personal stories detailing face-to-face encounters with ghosts and spirits to realize the paranormal is in fact quite normal! In writing this book I have been astounded by the consistency in the accounts given by those who have rubbed shoulders with the dead.

So how do you know you are in a haunted place?

It can be as subtle as a whisper, a sudden chill in an empty room, a quick evasive shadow momentarily glimpsed from the corner of the eye. A gentle nudging, a hint of perfume evoking a memory. A piece of music suddenly stirring you to tears.

I like to think a haunted place can be beautiful and restful. It doesn't need to be a fearful location steeped in a dark and troubled history. I like to think that many of the spirits we encounter are happy souls who just stayed too long at the fair.

My romantic notion was briskly shot down by psychic Shonali Thakur, who has had many close encounters with ghosts and hauntings all around the world.

"The idealists like to believe that," she told me curtly during our interview. "But sadly, haunted places can't be beautiful or peaceful. A haunted place means whoever lived there or died there didn't have a natural death. They are lingering here with unfinished business; they are lingering here troubled, unable to move on."

Read Shonali's hair-raising encounter with an evil spirit in the story of the haunted Holiday Inn in Rome.

Unfinished business is definitely a reason for a haunting. There is a stirring story about the murder victim who reaches out to his former partner Julian Jones in the hope he will help to solve the crime.

For Australian hair and makeup artist, Julian Jones, the spirit world is just as real if not more so than the physical. Julian has grown up with a spiritual gift that sees him interacting with the dead on a daily basis. Julian lives in a haunted house in a very haunted and haunting world.

"I initially hear noises, I definitely feel something," Julian says of his communing with ghosts. "It's like there's a train arriving. You know it's coming, you can feel it, you can hear it – you just can't see it at first."

Julian said he feels a bundle of confusion and fear when he feels the dead are first trying to reach him.

"I get a feeling on my skin, that weird feeling people describe as your skin crawling. I get this overriding feeling that someone is there, but I often can't see them at first.

"Sometimes it can be as simple as hearing their clothing rustle. It really is that analogy of waiting for the train to come, and for me, when it does, it's like being hit with the full force of a freight train. When it hits, it's an engulfing moment."

Children are very perceptive to haunted places. Research shows most children have the gift to see the spirit world. Those "imaginary friends" – which they often talk to and about – aren't imaginary! Sadly, the constraints of the adult "logical" world usually sees a child shutting that gift down by the time they reach five or six – leaving their imaginary friends behind. There must be many ghosts out there with issues of abandonment as a result of this!

One thing is certain: wherever we travel in the world, we are always going to be wandering in and out of haunted places.

And with haunted places come stories. Too many stories for one book.

This book has set out to throw the spotlight on many of the world's haunted places and tell the stories behind such locales. There is no rhyme nor reason to the places I've chosen, only the fact that the stories have grabbed my imagination and given me that hair-standing-on-end and goose-bumpy feel. The fact is, we all love a good scare.

Some of the stories are already famous and continue to be retold throughout the ages, others lesser known or not known at all. All are truly haunting. And some, although tinged with the paranormal, are downright inspirational.

I hope this book and the stories within can take you to a haunted place.

Happy haunting.

AOKIGAHARA – THE SUICIDE FOREST, JAPAN

"If you go down to the woods today
You're sure of a big surprise.
If you go down to the woods today
You'd better go in disguise!"

Yes, indeed.

And, if you go down to the Aokigahara woods in Japan, you will be sure of a big surprise and it won't be anything as happy as a Teddy Bear's Picnic!

Known as the Suicide Forest, this wooded hell-hole is without doubt one of the most chilling and haunted places in the world. It was the subject of the frightening horror movie, The Forest (2016) starring Natalie Dormer.

Those brave/mad enough to venture in are reported to have found clothing and body parts while strolling through the aptly named "sea of trees." This is a common occurrence: the clothing and body parts usually belong to the lost souls who enter the forest to end their lives.

It is estimated over a hundred suicides occur in the forest each year.

The Aokigahara woods, located at the base of Mount Fuji, plays a huge part in Japanese mythology. While it is known as the Suicide Forest, it is said, "Spirits cannot rest there, and they often come back angry."

The forest is regarded as the most haunted place in all of Japan with eyewitnesses and true believers of the paranormal experiencing excessive numbers of Yurei – ghosts who suffered violent and unnatural deaths. Many visitors with psychic gifts have said the place reeks of evil and is overridden with demonic forces.

"You have to guard your heart, protect yourself with white light, carry a bible or a cross if you want to come out of the forest sane and in one piece," warns Jamie Edmiston, a psychic healer who has been traversing the forest since the 1980s. She goes in hoping to help put lost souls trapped within the tangle of branches to rest.

The VICE documentary, *Aokigahara Suicide Forest,* takes a very up-close tour of the site seen through the eyes of Azusa Hayano, a geologist who works there. He is continuously aware that his daily work could see him happen across someone who has taken their own life or is about to.

The forest, 35 square kilometres in size, is a labyrinth of hemlock fir, Japanese cypress, Mongolian oak, Fuji Cherry and Maple trees – their roots knot and cluster across the forest floor in tripwire threads. The ground is uneven, rocky, and dotted with hundreds of caves. It is regarded as the perfect place to die as the moment you enter there is an overwhelming sense of isolation. The authorities are said to only search for bodies once a year as the forest is too dense to patrol on a regular basis.

As you wander the forest there is the detritus of countless suicide attempts including abandoned cars, tents, suicide notes and nooses. People say anyone entering the forest with a tent is obviously in two minds about whether or not they want to take their lives.

In the documentary, Havano points out the signposts that have been placed throughout the forest trying to dissuade the desperate and lost from going down the suicide path: "Your life is a precious gift from your parents. Please think about your parents, siblings and children."

Death by hanging is the most popular method of suicide among the Sea Of Trees. The second is said to be poisoning, usually by drug overdose.

In 1960, Japanese Writer Seicho Matsumoto's tragic novel *Kuroi Jukai*, was released. It told the story of a heartbroken lover who retreats to the Sea of Trees to end her life. This story seeped into Japanese culture and the Aokigahara Forest became the place to commit suicide. Another book. *The Complete Suicide Manual*, listed Aokigahara as "the perfect place to die." That book has often been found among the left-behind possessions of many visitors to the Suicide Forest.

It is said the place is cursed, with many of the dying leaving a curse on the world they are so desperate to leave behind. With so many curses uttered from the lips of the doomed, it is little wonder the place is a hive of ghostly and demonic activity.

Hikers and sightseers have reported hearing pained, unnatural screams while wandering the forest. They unanimously agree these screams are made by the Yurei (ghosts). A journalist for the Japan Times claimed he heard such a scream while he was traversing the forest for research. He went in search of the source of the scream and came across the dead body of a man at the base of a tree. The rotting corpse had clearly been there some time, so he could not have been the one who let out the terrifying scream. The reporter believes it was the man's spirit, tormented and not at rest.

Ghost sightings are frequent. There's almost as many reports of white figures drifting among the dense foliage as there are trees in the forest.

On a happier note, not everyone who tries to do away with themselves in the forest succeeds.

Hideo Watanabe owns a shop near the entrance to the forest. He has seen many a forlorn figure wandering defeated from the Sea of Trees after a failed suicide attempt.

He remembers one sad girl very vividly.

"She had tried to hang herself and failed," Hideo told the Japan Times. "She had part of the rope around her neck and her eyes were almost popping out of their sockets. I took her inside, made her some tea and called an ambulance."

Because Mount Fuji looms large over the forest, Aokigahara is regarded by most Japanese religions to be a very spiritual place. It is not unusual to find makeshift altars sharing the space with skulls and skeletons and withered corpses belonging to the dead. Many have mistakenly thought these corpses to have been sacrificed upon the altars by those dabbling in the Black Arts. This has proven to not be the case.

The altars usually belong to Buddhist monks who have erected their altars in the hope of trying to combat the evil spirits haunting the forest who taunt and beckon visitors to join them by also killing themselves.

Kyomyo Fukui is one such Buddhist monk devoted to cleansing the forest of any evil spirits. He spoke to the New Zealand Herald, who were doing a report on the forest.

"The spirits are calling people here to kill themselves," he told the paper as he busily went about setting up his altar in the Sea of Trees. "These are the spirits of the people who have committed suicide before."

It's as if good and evil are both drawn to the dense thicket of the Aokigahara Forest.

* * *

AUSCHWITZ, POLAND

The sign over the gates, "Arbeit Macht Frei" – (Work Sets You Free) is a blatant lie and a cruel joke. Unless of course the only way to be set free is to be worked to death, die in horror – your last days feeling terrified, tortured, starved, then gassed.

It must have been horrific being pushed and herded from those claustrophobic cattle cars to be met by merciless Nazi guards hell-bent on murder and enjoying the unrelenting fear and little hope they were offering. The whole time people being suddenly separated from their loved ones never to see them again. The electrified fences and the crazed Alsatians ensuring you had nowhere to run.

Walk through the gates of Auschwitz today and all those thoughts instantly rush to greet you. You can't help but be overcome by an all-consuming sense of sorrow. And the question that will haunt humanity forever: how could this have happened?

An eerie, but respectful silence pervades – no one wants to speak, or they are completely lost for words, often seeing the camp through a blur of tears.

Is Auschwitz haunted? How could it not be? This concentration camp is universally described as the worst of the worst. Here the Nazis terrorised, tortured and murdered 1.1 million victims. A place of unparalleled misery.

Those who visit the compound are instantly able to feel the unimaginable horrors, the unspeakable atrocities unleashed upon the vast array of innocent people sent to Auschwitz to be cruelly exterminated.

Many claim to hear screams, pleading cries for help. Others swear they have felt the grasp of a child's hand as if they are lost and want someone to help them find their mummy.

There is a pile of shoes, more like a mountain, thousands of shoes forced from the feet of the innocent. It's the hundreds of shoes once worn by children that cause most visitors to break down. And the piles of clothes, where the prisoners were forced to strip naked with no dignity before being forced to line up and look into the mass grave they were often forced to dig. Imagine their complete and overwhelming fear as they knew they too were soon to be part of that hellish hole containing the bleeding, twisted, bullet-shattered skulls and limbs of their loved ones.

Many visitors say they have felt very strong paranormal activity in the huts once overcrowded with emaciated prisoners, their gaunt frames so wasted they could barely stand and soon to find themselves fodder for the Gas Chambers.

"As I wandered through the barracks, you could only imagine how cold it was in winter, how bitterly cold and the Nazis not giving two hoots that people were freezing to death," says Ursula Thompson from Sydney, visiting Auschwitz for the third time to honor her Grandmother who never walked back through those gates with the lying message offering false hope.

"As I walked through the barracks where those poor people were overcrowded and diseased, I promise you I could see a very sad man in striped pajamas peering at me from one of those dreadful, threadbare bunks.

"Because he was now a skeleton, barely alive, his eyes seemed huge and he stared straight at me. I'll never forget those terribly sad, pleading eyes.

"When I went to talk to him, he just wasn't there anymore. I know what I saw."

Yes, Auschwitz is a haunted place and overrun with sadness and lost souls. There can be no denying.

But, it's also haunted by horrific ghouls so evil and sadistic they happily chose to work there and build their careers based around the misery of others.

Irma Grese, or "The Beautiful Beast" as she came to be known, flourished as a beyond-sadistic guard at Aushchwitz.

Her ghost, her dark energy, has been picked up on a regular basis by psychics and the spiritually sensitive.

An online article, *Are There Ghosts In Auschwitz?* published March 15, 2016, noted of Grese, "if ever there was proof that evil could exist within beauty, she was surely it."

Grese was born in Germany in 1923. Growing up had been difficult and she was, on the whole, unhappy. She was stunningly beautiful but socially inept. Her school life was lonely and she was relentlessly bullied and left isolated. The intense feeling of abandonment manifested more deeply when her mother committed suicide.

It is understood it was around this time she started taking a perverse interest in The Band Of German Maidens, a sinister umbrella of the Hitler Youth.

Grese took up her first role as a concentration camp guard in 1940. Her father pleaded with her not to go down this murderous path, but she flatly refused. Her father, deeply ashamed, completely disowned her.

Despite her mother committing suicide, Grese's father had brought her up well, instilling in her a moral backbone, but something overtook her and she chose to embrace the life of a hate-filled and murderous Nazi. She loved the power it seemed to give her. She relished the fear, hurt and torture she could inflict. She loved her free reign of terror.

All these "virtues" she could unleash when she was promoted to the ominous work/death camp, Auschwitz. Irma Grese, it can be said, must be one of the very few people in the world who relished being sent to Auschwitz.

It was as if this twisted sadist's dreams had all come true. She was placed in charge of terrorizing the 30,000 female Jewish prisoners.

"It was she who decided who was sent to the gas chamber and who survived, starving and degraded in the misery of the camp," *Are There Ghosts In Auschwitz?* (online article).

Having destroyed the lives of countless thousands, she went on to repeat her murderous performance at Bergen-Belsen in the closing months of the war.

Shortly after the war, as news of the unspeakable acts committed behind the wires of these camps came to light, Grese was arrested. The more the world heard about the horrors that went on in the likes of Auschwitz and Belsen, the more it recoiled and hung its head in shame.

Many couldn't wait to testify to the atrocities unleashed by Grese.

It was revealed she was the lover of the camp commander at Auschwitz and she was also involved sexually with the evil Dr. Mengele. She was said to have an insatiable love for sadistic sex.

It was revealed she owned a lampshade made from the skin of her slaughtered Jewish prisoners.

Grese was found guilty of her war crimes and was hanged at Hamelm Prison on 13 December 1945.

At the age of just 22 she had managed to pack so much evil and unrepentant murder and misery into such a young life.

She was the youngest woman to die judicially under British Law in the 20th Century. Grese was also the youngest of the concentration camp guards to be hanged.

She remained defiant even as the noose was being placed around her neck. She vowed she would return to haunt those who sentenced her to death.

Her ghost was first seen in 1948. An eyewitness saw her wandering near the gas chambers of Auschwitz. She wasn't true to her word. She didn't return to haunt those who hung her. Instead, she remained to wander through the camp where she once brought so much unspeakable sorrow.

Do the ghosts of those people who suffered at her cruel hand now turn on her, or is she left as she lived in her troubled youth, to wander alone and abandoned? Is Auschwitz now her hell like she made it for hundreds of thousands?

As the online article, *Are There Ghosts In Auschwitz?* proposed, "If you accept that ghosts exist where there has been great emotional turmoil, suffering and tragedy, then surely they must exist in Auschwitz."

* * *

BHANGARH FORT, INDIA

Built in 1573 in the district of Rajasthan, this imposing ancient ruin is considered India's most haunted place.

It casts a looming shadow from atop a hill and whether you approach it on the back of an elephant (as many tourists opt to do) or you speed towards it in a bumpy, hellish jeep ride, there is little doubt you are approaching a place of unbounded terror.

Bhangarh Fort, located between Jaipur and Alwar is definitely not for the easily spooked. The common catch cry among locals to visiting tourists is, "Don't you dare venture there after sunset." The place is said to be brimming with supernatural activity.

The hauntings can be traced back to the originator of the city, King Madho Singh. Singh was given approval to build the city after consulting with leading Guru Balu Nath, who meditated at the site. The Guru gave approval for the city to be built as long as the shadow of the emperor's palace would never touch him at his meditative retreat.

Sadly, the king's lust for power and riches overtook him. He first built his palace, then the Bhangarh Fort which was majestically high and imposing. The fort with its many stories cast long shadows and they crept over the incensed Guru Balu Nath.

Using his supernatural powers, the Guru went into a trance, his powerful thoughts sending out a destructive energy that destroyed the entire town. The curse is still there. Any attempt since to construct any buildings on the site have seen them quickly collapse.

The Guru is buried at the site of the fort and his ghost is said to torment and wander the ruins every day after sunset.

Adding to the fort's woes is another ancient curse that was put on the place by a demented, love-struck wizard.

According to folklore, a wizard named Singhia who lived in the town became besotted and obsessed with Ratnavati, the Princess of Bhangarh.

Knowing the princess was way above his lowly station, the wizard set about wooing her by using black magic. He put a spell on the oil the princess's maid was purchasing for the royal bath. He believed the princess would surrender her heart to him the moment she bathed in the oil.

The clever princess saw him perform his black magic spell, and upon receiving the oil she poured it on the ground. The oil turned into a giant rock and started rolling towards the shocked and frozen-to-the-ground magician. The rock rolled straight over the magician, crushing him.

Before succumbing to his horrific injuries, the magician cursed the Bhangarh city, saying there would be no more rebirths.

Shortly after the curse was called, there was a bloody battle between Bhangarh and Ajabgarh, which saw Princess Ratnavati assassinated. However, some stories tell that the princess has taken a rebirth somewhere else and the Bhangarh Fort is waiting for her return to end the sadistic curse.

The fort's main entrance is locked and the government has placed a notice board at the main gate which reads that "Visiting the fort before sunrise and after sunset is strictly prohibited."

Many superstitious government authorities and locals believe that spirits roam in Bhangarh Fort at night. People often hear strange noises - screaming, crying voices of women, bangles clanking in the rooms. Others report hearing voices whispering in urgent sounding tones and sudden strong traces of exotic perfumes. There have been reports of phantom bands playing music and the sounds of people gaily dancing. But the moment the sun rises, all falls quiet on the mysterious Bangarh Fort.

* * *

CAPE LEEUWIN LIGHTHOUSE, AUSTRALIA

The Cape Leeuwin Lighthouse is situated at the most south-westerly tip of Australia, standing at the point where the Indian and Southern Oceans meet.

Its piercing beam is as intense as one million candles and can be seen for 48 kilometers.

Spare a thought for the lighthouse keepers who through the years had to climb the 186 steps four times a day to ensure the light kept burning. Such was life at the remote Cape Leeuwin Lighthouse that has been standing tall, a guardian of the ocean, since 1895.

Modern times finally caught up with the limestone tower and the Lighthouse was automated in September 1992.

Time may have moved on, but a certain Lighthouse Keeper's wife refused to budge. She is the ghost who dwells in Cottage Three, the cottage closest to the historical lighthouse.

Photographer Peter Rigby has been photographing the Lighthouse for years. Normally a skeptic when it comes to the paranormal, Peter is convinced there is definitely a presence in Cottage Three.

"When I go to the Lighthouse, I know I can feel her," Peter says. "There is a sense of desolation in the cottage and it certainly is colder than the other ones."

The story goes that one day in 1909, the then Lighthouse Keeper's wife Maud Elizabeth Govett Miner was heavily pregnant. She was cleaning up the house in preparation of her baby's arrival. She stood on a chair to adjust a curtain, suffered a heavy fall and injured herself very badly.

Sadly, due to the isolation of the Lighthouse, it took days for the doctor to arrive. It was too late.

"She died from septicaemia and tragically her baby died too," Peter explains. "They were just too far from anywhere. You have to remember Cape Leeuwin is the most south-westerly point of Western Australia.

"She was obviously a much-loved lady because 30 years after her death they were still placing a memorial notice on the anniversary of her passing in the West Australian newspaper."

And since her passing, Cottage Three, where she was living at the time, has been a constant source of haunted activity.

"Strange things go on out there," Pete says with much understatement. "The current Lighthouse Caretaker and Tours Supervisor, Paul Sofilas, has lived on site for 10 years; he talks of lights going on and off for no reason. Doors will open and close and no one is there.

"According to Paul, pregnant women, women with prams, women with young babies are particularly drawn to Cottage Three. The staff out there say these sorts of women get really emotional when passing Cottage Three without even knowing the story of the Lighthouse Keeper's wife.

"It's as if the Lighthouse Keeper's wife is beckoning them so she can see their babies. She was very maternal; she had three other children and she didn't get to give birth to her much-anticipated fourth child. Many say the loss of that baby would be the reason why her spirit has not been able to move on. It's amazing that pregnant women and women with young babies feel her presence most acutely."

There was one woman passing by the cottage on her way to the Lighthouse when she saw a woman in period dress standing on the veranda of Cottage Three. She came running back to the office to report what she had seen.

"The office staff took her back to the cottage and showed her a photograph of the Lighthouse Keeper's wife that is kept in the lounge room," Peter explains. "The woman screamed and almost fainted. 'It was her,' she gasped. 'I just saw her standing there on the balcony.' How do you explain that?"

No one can explain it. But, the maternal presence of the ghostly Lighthouse Keeper's wife keeps the tourists flocking to the wild isolation of the Cape Leeuwin Lighthouse.

* * *

CRITERION HOTEL, AUSTRALIA

Australia's Most Haunted Pub: "Don't go into Room 9"

Downstairs in the dimly lit back room of a Queensland bar, a team of paranormal experts are setting up technical equipment in the hopes of recording a haunting.

Evening shadows have already come creeping in, and outside this imposing 1860s former boarding house, a historical lamplight casts eerie shadows against the walls.

Welcome to the Criterion Hotel on Wharf Street, Maryborough, in Queensland Australia. It's a cold Friday evening and the Paranormal Paratek team, led by ghost enthusiast, Darren Davies, are wiring the extensive rooms of this rambling building with light sensors, microphones, digital audio recorders and infrared cameras.

It's time-consuming, hard work, made even harder by Darren – a merchant navy seaman – who is a perfectionist and a demanding taskmaster. He needs to be, as Paranormal Paratek's motto is "Seeking truth by evidence".

Susan Bowes, Scott Hynde and Shane Daly form the remainder of the team. They are quick to point out they loathe the term "ghostbuster" and take their work very seriously.

"There are two types of haunting," Darren says. "Residual or intelligent. A residual haunting can be a noise like breathing, the sound of footsteps on a staircase, scents like a cigar or talcum powder.

"An intelligent haunting is interactive. You get timely answers to questions asked, doors opening or closing, objects moving."

THERE IS LITTLE DOUBT ROOM 9 HAS A PRESENCE
Here in this shadowy pub, the team are hoping tonight will bring

about the emergence of the former caretaker, Ian Kennedy. His ghost is said to loom upstairs in the room at the end of the corridor – Room 9, where he died.

Ian was said to be a rather narky character while alive and is equally cantankerous in his spirit form. He and Darren have had several run-ins over the years. Darren recalls that one time he entered Room 9 and distinctly heard a thunderous, wildly angry voice telling him to "Get out!"

As he sets up a TV monitor that's trained on the mysterious Room 9, Darren explains what he does to prepare for a ghostly encounter.

"The best way to experience something paranormal is to find quiet time alone in a particular area, clear the mind and just wait," he says. "This normally works for me."

He dares me to experience the room myself, I furtively climb the darkened stairs that lead to a foreboding corridor of abandoned bedrooms. The moment my feet hit the top landing and my eyes struggle to adjust to the gloom, the temperature drops, and as I walk into Room 9 I am overcome with headaches. This is not a pleasant room.

Is it my imagination playing tricks? Do I genuinely feel unwell, and do I really hear a sinister whisper telling me to get out? Either way, I soon scurry back down the corridor.

"That always happens," declares Paratek's secretary, Susan Bow, or Psychic Suze as the team fondly call her. "I'm the only one who can go into Room 9 without being overcome by nausea and headaches. I always ask permission first and bathe myself in white light before going in. I like to go in and talk to Ian Kennedy.

"I'm someone who has never feared the dead. Growing up, people thought I was a bit strange."

Susan does have an intense stare. Perhaps she's seeing a parallel world at the same time she is engaging with you in the present. Her outlook is completely different from Darren's practical "show me the physical proof" approach.

IT'S GOING TO BE A LONG NIGHT

Downstairs in a secluded dark corner, Darren has set up a portrait of a white-bearded Ian Kennedy on the bar. This was Ian's favorite spot in the pub.

Alongside the portrait sits an old oil lamp and keys that belonged to him. "Personal trinkets," the team tell us, "will often entice spirits to manifest."

The night is long, but finally we do experience some strange and chilling happenings. As the team settle into their work, Darren bravely returns to Room 9.

"I know you decide when you want to make yourself known," he says into the darkness. "But can you do it now?"

And he hears a voice clear as day return, "OK."

The sound of shuffling feet follows and vibration sensors start going off.

What follows next leaves us all floored. He calls to the dark, "I am here for you, Ian, or anybody else who may be here."

And this time, a distinctive female voice calls back from the shadows, "Thank you."

Darren's certainly not alone! Does the arrival of the female voice mean that the mysterious Room 9 houses two ghostly guests?"

Susan smiles mysteriously. As if she's known this for some time.

"When it comes to ghosts, to haunted places, people are left to form their own opinions," she says. "It is something you have to experience first-hand to fully believe and understand."

As for the living guests, the regulars who crowd the Criterion's bar to down spirits rather than conjure them up, they love sharing the haunted space.

"It's not scary," says Tricia Hughes, visiting from Sydney. "A couple of ghosts can only add to the atmosphere. As long as they're friendly."

❖ Criterion Rockhampton, Queensland ❖
Criterion is the criteria for a haunting

Ghosts must be drawn to pubs named Criterion, for while the patrons at the Criterion in Maryborough are feeling spooked, another Queensland watering hole of the same name also has its demons.

Here in its lofty rooms overlooking the Fitzroy River in the central Queensland city of Rockhampton, ceiling fans swish through the damp, heavy-hanging air of the tropics.

An imposing staircase, its gilded banisters well-worn and polished by the countless hands that have clasped them through the ages leads to more high-ceilinged rooms. Even when the staircase appears empty, patrons and staff insist they can hear footsteps traipsing down in a scuffed manner.

People started talking about the Criterion being haunted back in the 1980s. One night a young barman, Peter Hudson, was locking up. He had just locked and bolted the door leading to the grand old Riverview Room and walked across the lobby. He turned back to notice the door he had just locked was now hanging open. Peter shook his head but thought nothing more of it and continued with his closing-up duties.

He moved on to the kitchen and adjoining laundries. He was passing an old servants' stairway when he felt a sudden chill in the air.

He turned, consumed with fear, startled and gasping. There in the doorway stood a woman in a long, old-fashioned dress wearing lace-up boots with her hair piled on top of her head. The odd thing was, he could see the old brickwork of the pub through her dress. It was as if he were watching an old movie projected onto the wall.

Peter stood staring at the apparition for a good 20 seconds and the ghost stared brazenly back at him. He said he felt frozen to the spot, but when he could finally get his body into gear he fled the scene with a mixture of fear and total bewilderment. He forced himself to go back to the room only to see the woman turning a corner and vanishing down a corridor.

Who the woman is remains the key topic of conversation among the regular crowd and staff at the Criterion.

Some say it's the ghost of a young prostitute murdered in one of the upstairs rooms last century, others think it's the former owner who died at the pub a few years after it opened in 1889.

In its glory days, the Criterion played host to the who's who of Queensland. Sir Charles Kingsford Smith slept there. In World War II, it was taken over by the Americans and General Douglas MacArthur occupied one of the best suites.

The regular housekeeping staff have no doubt the Criterion is a haunted place. Housemaids say that often when they make a bed, a few moments later the bedspread will have moved and there is an indentation where someone has been sitting even though no one but the housekeeper has been in the room. And the kitchen staff, not far from the staircase where the mysterious lady was first spotted, all claim to feel "chills" and "a presence" when they pass by the stairs.

And while the kitchen area is prone to plunges in temperature, out in the front bar the air remains thick with humidity and the ever-turning ceiling fans labor to generate even the faintest of breezes. It's obvious the ghost hasn't yet ventured into this part of the Criterion. If she did, all would be aware of her "cool" presence and there would be no need for ceiling fans.

* * *

GHOSTS OF THE EIFFEL TOWER
AND OTHER PARTS OF PARIS, FRANCE

It may be the city of lights, a romantic's dream where you can't help but fall in love. But stroll anywhere in Paris and you will find death lingers near.

This stunning wonder upon the River Seine is truly a haunted city. Some call it the city of love. It's also a place where the dead love to dwell!

It seems in Paris, love and death stroll hand in hand.

There is a female ghost – the victim of a fractured love affair – that haunts Level One of the Eiffel Tower.

The story goes, a pair of young lovers had arranged to meet at their favorite romantic meeting place – Level One of the Eiffel Tower.

He, an American in Paris, had spruced himself up, bought roses, and tucked an engagement ring inside his freshly pressed suit coat. This was the day he was going to propose to the love of his life.

She, a girl from Montmartre, had nervously approached the Tower, stopping beneath a Chestnut tree to powder her nose and wipe away a tear. This was the day she was going to break it off with the man she no longer loved.

The moment he saw her exit the lift, her face forlorn, he knew this was not going to be the happiest day of his life like he'd envisaged. He couldn't believe his ears as she falteringly told him: it was over.

His pride and ego, dashed. He couldn't believe he had just been dumped. He became enraged. It is believed he either pushed or threw her over the side of the tower. She plunged 57 meters to her death.

Since that fateful day, visitors to Level One claim to have heard the same sequence of sounds in the very spot where the woman fell.

At first they hear a female giggling, then the giggle turns to an argumentative plea. Then terrified screams ring out. The spooky thing, is the same sequence is always reported.

This was a tragic murder, but the Eiffel Tower has long been a magnet for suicides. It's the great unspoken. Sadly, it's still a very common place to attempt to commit suicide in Europe. Hence, it's one of the most haunted places in Europe.

Russian Princess Anna Troubetzkoy is one of the most famous to hurl herself from the tower.

Anna was on honeymoon, having just married a man known as Prince Serge in New York. The love birds seemed happy when they hit Paris. They were going to be there for a few days before making their way through Europe to Russia where they would renew their vows in August 1931.

But, something snapped in Anna's brain. While atop the tower, she turned to her new husband and famously shouted the words, "So sorry to rain on your parade," then quickly hurled herself over the edge.

She meant her words literally. She fell amid a parade celebrating Bastille Day beneath the tower that fateful July 14, 1931.

Her death was initially ruled accidental, but shortly after a suicide/ farewell note was found in her bag.

Each Bastille Day, visitors to the top of the Eiffel Tower have reported hearing a mysterious voice shout out, "So sorry to rain on your parade." But when they turn to see who is shouting the words, there is no one there.

❖ The Most Beautiful Corpse In History ❖

She is the personification of serenity. During the bitter winter of 1880, the body of a young girl was dragged from the River Seine in the shadow of the Louvre.

She was a picture of ultimate peace. Her face unscarred, she didn't appear to have any injuries at all.

The morticians at the Paris morgue were so taken by her beauty that they made a death mask of her. Her face became an instant sensation with all of Paris. And because she had been found floating right near the Louvre, she was dubbed the "Mona Lisa of the Seine".

Her death was not in vain. Her face became the model for the first

CPR dummy which remains in use today. She is often called "the most kissed girl in the world". In death she has managed to receive the kiss of life millions of times over. Many claim that when they approach the portrait of the Mona Lisa in the Louvre, the young girl's face suddenly appears in the painting.

❧ He Haunts The Catacombs ❧

In 1793, a man hell bent on theft entered the pitch-black Paris catacombs. Philihert Aspairt had planned to make his way through the labyrinth of darkness and end up in the wine cellar of a nearby convent. He was longing to taste some Chartreuse Liquor.

Sadly, he lost his way when his candle suddenly went out. His bones were found 11 years later. He was only identifiable by the set of keys found next to his skeleton.

Every November 3, it is said his ghost awakens to wander the catacombs. Visitors have heard him whispering in their ears before he snuffs out their candles. He is now referred to as the Saint of the Catacombs. It has become a tradition for terrified visitors who encounter the ghost to have a drink of Chartreuse Liquor in his honor after they leave the catacombs.

❧ The Most Haunted Street In Paris ❧

There is something palpably eerie about Rue des Chantres. Parisians all agree it is the most haunted street in the city, and one with a tragic past.

During the 1900s, sick children with consumption were confined in a section of the Hôtel-Dieu located on this street, to keep them from infecting the rest of Paris.

A record flood saw the River Seine overflow and the children, locked in their rooms, were unable to escape. Every single child drowned.

People walking down the Rue des Chantres feel chilled and terrified as they hear the screams of the children, and sometimes their playful laughter. Many have seen the shadows of spectral children playing in the tiny courtyard at the base of the street.

THE GHOST OF EVA PERON - HER BIZARRE TRIP AS AN EMBALMED CORPSE, ARGENTINA

"Oh what a circus, Oh what a show.
Argentina has gone to town,
Over the death of an actress called Eva Peron."
Che Guevara in the musical Evita.

The death of Eva Peron took Argentina's First Lady from working class hero to eternal saint. Her lavish State funeral, the grandest ever staged in the turbulent country, went on for days.

As Che would go on to sing in the West End musical, "We've all gone crazy, mourning all day and mourning all night. Falling over ourselves to get all of the misery right."

The charismatic, glamorous second wife of Argentina's late President, Juan Peron, succumbed to cancer at age just 33.

At 8:25pm July 26 1952, the lights in her bedroom inside the grand Casa Rosada, Government House Buenos Aires dimmed and then were switched off. Evita Peron was dead.

Word of Evita's passing spread within minutes and hysterical, grief-stricken Argentinians, desperate to express their anguish, hurled themselves into the streets.

It was hardly surprising that even in death, Eva Peron would not be allowed to rest. Her loving followers, the ones she called her "Descamisados," (the Shirtless Ones), just could not and would not let her go.

It's also hardly surprising, due to the harrowing last months of her life and the bizarre weeks of grieving following her passing, Evita, like many troubled spirits would reappear to many of her followers. Not only was she a Saint, she was now a ghost.

She was famous and loved for her charismatic speeches, given from behind a bank of glinting microphones on the balcony of the

Casa Rosada. She'd be dressed up to the nines, wearing the latest Christian Dior and holding out her arms from the balcony to embrace her loving shirtless ones below.

There is a famous picture of her at the height of her glamour, a picture of sophistication and radiant health, the style icon embracing her followers with a regal wave. That picture was taken in October 1950.

Eerily, not long after her passing, people began reporting a strange woman dressed elegantly in white, striding the balcony of her beloved Casa Rosada. The eyewitnesses have all said this woman had the same hairstyle as Evita. She turned to wave, smiled then she was gone. Hundreds of people have reported the same sighting. It is as if this spectral figure is locked in that triumphant day of October 1950.

Workers within the Casa Rosada have also reported the ghostly sightings of Evita. They have seen her both on the balconies and sweeping along the majestic corridors of the vast presidential palace.

In May 2012, a tourist filming the outside of the Casa Rosada captured footage of the so-called Woman in White. The ghostly image of the woman ethereal and fleeting on the second story balcony caused a worldwide sensation. True believers were convinced they were seeing an apparition of their beloved Santa Evita.

Many skeptics, to be expected, dismissed the haunting image as an elaborate hoax enhanced by the wonders of computer technology.

It has recently come to light that Evita underwent a prefrontal lobotomy to relieve the pain and anxiety she famously suffered in her last months. This left her in a state of permanent sedation, many claiming she would not have been aware of her surroundings. The bizarre medical procedure was said to have been carried out by an American surgeon, James L Poppen, who earned the nickname, "The Great Lobotomist." Her suffering may have been numbed by the operation, but Evita at the time of her passing was an emaciated wreck – a shell of her once high-spirited, beautiful self.

The troubled way she died leaves believers in the paranormal saying Eva Peron would have had trouble leaving her earthly surrounds and glory days as Argentina's First Lady.

"The Casa Rosada is definitely a haunted place," says former

Buenos Aires resident Mabelle Peters. "I remember as a girl being told never to linger outside or look up at the balcony because you don't know what you're going to encounter.

"I used to run past the place. One day I did stop. And I was sure I saw a sad lady looking out of the window, looking down at me. She was dressed in white. She seemed sad and troubled. I know I felt terrified. I do believe I glimpsed the ghost of Eva Peron."

Her bizarre afterlife ensured the spirit of Eva Peron would have been troubled.

In preparation for her State Funeral, Eva's corpse was embalmed by the highly acclaimed Spanish embalmer, Dr Pedro Ara. Ara was said not to like being called an embalmer and preferred to be regarded as an expert in the "art of death."

Ara initially prepared Eva's body only for the much-called-for public viewing, but he grossly underestimated the mass grief gripping the country. People went into a frenzy wanting to see their Evita. More than 2 million people filed past the body of Eva Peron and this outpouring of grief dragged on for weeks.

Fed up, Ara demanded Juan Peron to call a halt. He insisted he had to get on with his art. The second embalming of Evita was meant to last forever and her corpse would feature in an elaborate monument her husband was planning in her honor. The plan was for Evita to loom larger than life itself over the people of Argentina. Juan Peron wanted the monument to be bigger than the Statue of Liberty.

By the time Ara had completed his Art of Death on the body of Evita, at a whopping cost of over $100,000 and taking a ridiculous two years, devotees of the First Lady were no longer sure it was their idol, but rather a surreal statue.

The monument stalled with the throwing over of the Peron regime in 1955. Peron went into exile and Eva's corpse mysteriously went missing.

The story of Evita's missing corpse, which lasted close to 20 years, is so incredibly bizarre you could not make it up.

Being the symbol of Peronism, the generals who staged the coup had to make her disappear. The shirtless ones may have loved their Evita, but the new regime certainly didn't.

It's truly a macabre journey. It's said her body spent time in a van casually parked in the streets of Beunos Aires. Pedestrians walking by the van could never have known the body of their beloved saint was lying ignominiously inside. She was then stashed behind a cinema screen and ended her days in Buenos Aires in the city's waterworks and then in the offices of Military Intelligence.

But was the ghost of Evita still reaching out to those who loved her? Someone knew of her strange voyage because wherever her embalmed body was stashed, there would suddenly appear lit candles and flowers.

According to a report by BBC Radio 4 journalist, Linda Presley, Evita's embalmed corpse, with the assistance of the Vatican, was taken to a Milan cemetery and buried under a false name.

But The Argentinians could not forget their First Lady. She became a symbol of resistance. Graffiti would suddenly appear on the streets of Buenos Aires overnight, demanding, "Where is the body of Eva Peron?"

In 1970, Peronist backers kidnapped and killed General Pedro Eugenio Aramburu. He was blamed for the initial disappearance of Evita's corpse.

The Peronist Party was legalized again and Evita's well-travelled body would be returned to her widower, who had remarried and was living in Exile in Spain.

Evita was dug up, driven across Europe and dropped off at Peron's, where he was living with his third wife, Isabel, in Madrid.

The trip had taken its toll on Evita; she arrived at Juan's with a broken nose and blows to her face and chest. But then again, the poor thing had been pulled from pillar to post. One of her fingers was missing. This had been cut off by the military after the 1955 coup. They wanted to verify they actually had the right corpse.

It sounds incredibly macabre and fantastic, but it is reported that Juan and Isabel would even have the corpse of Evita with them in their dining room while they were enjoying their evening meal.

Incredibly, it was Isabel who spent much of her time tending to and cleaning up Eva's disheveled body. How many third wives would do that for their husbands?

In 1973, Peron was restored as President of Argentina and Isabel became his Vice-President. Evita had always yearned for that role.

Sadly, Juan died the following year and Isabel became president. Another dream of Eva's. And it was the kind-hearted Isabel who made sure Evita's body would finally be brought home to Argentina.

Eva's remains were again worked on and restored, this time by Domingo Tellechea.

But another coup was imminent and in 1976, Isabel Peron was deposed and chaos ensued. Thousands would flee into exile or suddenly disappear.

Ironically, it was the military who oversaw the final burial of Eva Peron in October 1976 in the very wealthy and refined Recoleta cemetery, surrounded by all the wealthy families who had despised her.

Her crypt is the most visited. Each day hordes of visitors come with their flowers and cards to pay homage to Evita.

The military, it is believed, buried her five meters underground in a crypt "fortified like a military bunker". They presumed no one would ever be able to interfere with her remains ever again.

But judging by the number of impromptu appearances of her ghost – many times strolling the grounds of the Recoleta cemetery and many times seen waving to the crowds from the Casa Rosada, the ghost of Eva Peron cannot be contained, sealed up, or fenced in.

* * *

GHOSTS AT A GLANCE – LONG ISLAND'S STEADY FLOW OF SPOOKS, UNITED STATES

Don't Rankle Mrs. Sweeney (Long Island New York)

New York: Jan Oosting, his wife Kathleen and their five kids present as your "normal" American family – that is until you add their "uninvited" guest, Mrs. Sweeney, to the mix.

"Mrs. Sweeney" is the name the Oostings have bestowed upon the ghostly presence who lingers in their hundred-year-old farmhouse along Old Stump Road, Brookhaven, Long Island. They staunchly believe a cantankerous Mrs. Sweeney was responsible for a hand mirror inexplicably being hurled across a bedroom before smashing to the floor and shattering into a million pieces.

But she isn't always cranky. Most of the time Mrs. Sweeney is happy to appear simply as a floating head above a lamp in the lounge room or a wispy figure waving from the upstairs veranda.

All of the Oosting family have experienced an encounter with Mrs. Sweeney in all of her manifestations.

Jan Oosting, who was a science teacher and former researcher at an atomic energy laboratory, was at a loss to offer a rational explanation for their ghost.

But Kathleen and the five Sweeney children all believe Mrs. Sweeney, who often appears as a gentle old woman standing only five feet tall, with grey hair neatly tied in a bun, is the ghost of a farmer's wife who lived in their farmhouse at the turn of the century.

THE OVERPASS OF DEATH
Long Island is prolific with ghosts and haunted places. Those

passing beneath the Northern State Parkway overpass tell of feeling suddenly overcome with a sense of dread and horror.

It is said several teenagers banded together to commit a mass suicide by hanging themselves from the overpass. Legend has it that if you honk your car horn three times while driving beneath the overpass you can suddenly see their lifeless bodies.

Others report seeing a troubled soul known as the Lady In White lingering near the overpass. It is believed she is a former psychiatric patient who, while in a depressed state, burned the Long Island Hospital down. She also reportedly lost her life in the blaze.

But other locals beg to differ about the identity of the so-called Lady In White. Some call her Mary who was either hit by a car or murdered on the road. Whoever she is, she is there. There are too many sightings to doubt it.

A crying child can be heard beckoning over the steady stream of traffic along Long Island's Sweet Hollow Road. The mutilated body of a unidentified child was discovered on that road in 1976. The body remains nameless and the murder unsolved.

KINGS PARK PSYCHIATRIC CENTRE, KINGS PARK

Built in 1885 and sprawling over more than 800 acres of land, Kings Park Psychiatric Centre has been described as a "Mini city of restless, anguished souls."

Kings Park was once home to more than 9,000 mentally-unhinged patients. Amid the 150 buildings including a library, a firehouse, morgue and cemetery, the patients were subjected to electric shock therapy, insulin shock therapy, and prefrontal lobotomies. It was a grim place of ceaseless torment and uncompromising terror.

And while the grisly procedures carried out there (often in secret and behind locked doors) have long ceased and the buildings fallen into disrepair, passersby often report hearing screams, moans, banging and clanging. These chilling sounds all serve as a constant reminder of the pain and anguish suffered by the countless patients who found themselves committed to the guaranteed horrors of Kings Park Psychiatric Centre. If you weren't mad when you first went in, it was said you would be by first light the next day.

The walls of Kings Park have witnessed and hidden countless inhuman atrocities of torture and abuse. It's little wonder it is renowned as a very haunted place.

WICKHAM FARMHOUSE, CUTCHOGUE LONG ISLAND, NEW YORK

Built in 1704, Wickham Farmhouse is one of the oldest English-style abodes in New York State. But despite its benign appearance, the farmhouse became a brutal crime scene with the vicious slaying of James and Frances Wickham, along with their 14-year-old servant boy, who were all brutally murdered in their beds.

Asleep in the dark in the early hours of June 2 1854, all three were hacked to death by an axe-wielding maniac, a 21-year-old farmhand named Nicholas Behan.

Screams of terror and pleading calls for help can still be heard as people pass by the farmhouse today. Many years after the dreadful murders, in 1988, descendants of James and Frances Wickham were visiting the farmhouse and staying over.

It is reported that during the course of their stay, they were woken in the night to find a ghost of a man standing menacingly over their bed. Was it the ghost of Nicholas Behan? It is strongly believed that is the case. An axe has often been found left menacingly by the front door of the farmhouse.

Shortly after the ghostly visitation, the bedroom was reportedly sealed off and no one has ventured into that room since.

THE NORMANDIE INN, SMITHTOWN AND LAKELAND AVENUE, BOHEMIA, LONG ISLAND

It was originally built for a Czech baron in the 1920s. The prohibition era saw it transformed into a crime-riddled Speakeasy frequented by gangsters. It then took on grandiose airs and graces by becoming the Hotel Chateau La Boheme. Its final personality change happened when it became a simple restaurant.

Falling down and a mere shadow of its glory days, the Gothic-style structure has been boarded up since 2004. It is up for sale again but stories of the place being overrun by a troubled ghost often turn would-be buyers away.

The Normandie Inn is said to be haunted by a murder victim simply known as Maria. Maria was allegedly strangled to death in an upstairs back bedroom. Her ghost was often heard walking the hallways and knocking on visitors' doors when the building was still a hotel. There have been reports of apparitions in darkened hallways and cold spots in certain rooms upstairs. More chillingly, long-silent room service bells have been heard to start ringing without explanation and footprints once appeared on a just-shampooed rug in a locked bedroom.

REID ICE CREAM GROUNDS, ATLANTIC AVENUE, BLUE POINT, LONG ISLAND

And while the ghost of Maria continues to ring for room service, a little ways up the road someone is screaming for ice cream.

In 1966, the body of a murdered 20-year-old go-go dancer and part time bank teller was discovered in the sump of the Reid Ice Cream Grounds. Her hands and feet were bound, her throat had been savagely slashed. Locals say the woman has never left the once-happy Ice Cream Grounds. Faint traces of Go-Go music have often been heard playing at night then suddenly halting with the terrified screams of a woman.

* * *

GHOSTS OF GALLIPOLI AND WW1

You only have to stand on the shores of Gallipoli in the dark early morning quiet to know you are standing in a hallowed and haunted place.

Beautiful and moving, horrific and yet so peaceful at the same time. There is a beckoning presence, almost soothing as if to say forget the blood of slaughter, the carnage of our winless battles, we are now at peace.

Psychics who visit the place in their droves agree the ghosts of Gallipoli are mostly at peace and certainly benevolent.

In town, the locals will tell you Gallipoli definitely has its ghosts. They speak of screams in the night which echo around the cliffs and off the water.

"They are not the screams of ANZAC Day revelers who gather there in their thousands," says a sturdy, weather-beaten barman named Aziz. "No, these screams ring out in the dead of night when the ANZAC day crowd have all gone back home. My friend Renee, who believes in ghosts, says she has often seen strange lights flickering out in the place they call No Man's Land.

"And there's too many others who have heard the yelling and screams for there not to be something there."

Many argue that the famous battlefields of World War I are not haunted as they have been subject to memorials and funerals and last rites where the dead have been laid to rest and are no longer lost and wandering and unwittingly "haunting" their place of death.

Australian photographer Joe Armao reignited the argument when he took a series of stirring photographs at Beach Cemetery at Hell Spit, one of the battlefields of Gallipoli.

Armao was in the company of a local guide and author Celal Boz and journalist Tony Wright. There was no one else present as dusk was quickly turning to night.

He had just taken his last series of pictures for the day and in those last frames, had captured something stirring and inexplicable. Armao couldn't believe his eyes when he went to examine his last three frames a few seconds after shooting them.

The shadowy silhouette of a figure, his back turned from the camera, and wearing a wide-brimmed Digger's hat appeared in the frame.

What was even stranger, the ghostly figure appears in only one of a series of three near-identical frames shot by Armao over 40 seconds. Armao said the camera angle had changed no more than 15 centimeters over the series of pictures, and the shutter had been set for a 2-3 second exposure due to the onset of dark.

Reporter Tony Wright, recounting the incident for the Fairfax Media, said, "He could offer no explanation, but he said the hair stood up on the back of his neck. When he showed Celal and me, we packed up and left the empty cemetery."

Tony said hours of close and skeptical inspection of the frame ensued as well as lively discussions involving theories of shadows and tricks of light and movement of the camera during the 2.5 second exposure.

"All that offered no explanation," he said. "It was simply a moment in a darkening graveyard, 99 years since Anzac soldiers stormed ashore at nearby Anzac Cove, captured by a closing shutter."

Tony said it was up to the reader to decide.

We may be experiencing ghostly encounters 100 plus years after World War 1, but back then, in the midst of battle as the war was dragging on, specters seemed to abound.

Official War Artist William Orpen, while painting his masterpiece Somme Battlefield, encountered a "strange force."

In November 1917, Orpen was painting in Thiepval Wood. It was 18 months after the Battle of Somme. Today that same wood has a monument dedicated to missing soldiers of the Somme. Upon the monument are the names of 73,376 British and Commonwealth soldiers who have no known grave.

"When Orpen was painting his Somme work, there were still many bodies scattered about him. Despite 18 months having passed since the battle, the place was still sprinkled in human remains.

The artist would later recall "a strange sense of presence which persisted". He had been painting for a couple of hours. "The sun was still shining, but the day was dark," Orpen said he was overwhelmed by feelings of dread and fear. He was sitting by a bullet-blasted, shattered trunk of a blackened tree, when something seemed to rush at him.

Orpen said he could see nothing but found himself flung backwards, hitting his head heavily on the ground. Then whatever it was, was gone.

The artist, panic-stricken, struggled to his feet before realizing his canvas had been destroyed. It had smashed to the ground and eerily, an unknown soldier's skull had ripped through the center of the canvas. Orpen wrote about this experience in his book, *An Onlooker In France 1917-1919* (1921, 2008).

The ghostly encounter and the symbol of the deceased soldier's skull made his final work, Somme Battlefield, all the more powerful.

Ironically, a popular password used by British soldiers early in the war was the word "Ghosts." And the soldiers were experiencing their own sightings.

The amount of death surrounding them, the carnage of war, made many service men and women superstitious and open to the supernatural.

The poet Robert Graves had commented on the growing phenomena of ghost spotting and superstition in his classic poem *Goodbye To All That*. He had written that people were open to "believing in signs of the most trivial nature."

But Graves himself had had his own run in with a phantom. He had been dining with army buddies at a café in Bethune in June 1915.

He was startled when glancing up from the meal to see his old friend and fellow solider, Private Challoner of the Royal Welch, looking in the window of the café. Private Challoner smiled, saluted those gathered at table then moved away. Graves instantly jumped up from the table and ran outside to greet his friend. Looking around, he found nothing but a smoking cigarette butt.

"I could not mistake him or the cap badge he wore," a shaken Graves said. "Yet no Royal Welch battalion was billeted within miles of Bethune at the time."

And there was also the fact Grave's dear chum had been killed at Festubert in May 1915.

Prior to his death, just before they left England, Private Challoner had said to Graves, "I'll see you in France, sir."

Was his phantom appearance at the café window just him remaining true to his word? Perhaps Graves found out when he went to his grave in 1985.

THE ANGELS OF MONS

Did a band of angels suddenly appear and save the British and Allied forces from certain defeat during the Battle of Mons in 1914.

Eyewitnesses insisted that is indeed what happened.

Midway through the disastrous and grueling battle, the German cavalry suddenly retreated from one part of the battlefield despite having the upper hand. This unexpected retreat gave the Allies a chance to take cover and avoid more unnecessary and tragic loss of life.

It is said that word quickly spread among the soldiers that "angel-like" apparitions had come down between the two opposing sides. The angels shielded the Allies and terrifying the Germans into a hasty retreat.

Word of the angelic intervention spread like wildfire. Was it a band of angels or ghosts of dead soldiers who came to fight the good fight?

The incident was reported in the British Press. The Daily Mail, in an interview with Private Robert Clever of the 1st Cheshire Regiment, recounted the battle and story of the mysterious angels. Clever had been an eyewitness to the phenomenon.

Clever described the Angels as "supernatural visions".

The paper said, "Suddenly the vision came between them and German cavalry. Private Cleaver described it as 'a flash'…"

This incident showed to many that war was not something restricted to the ways and wills of mankind, that is could also be played out beyond the here and now, its course changed by forces from the spiritual realm.

* * *

HOLIDAY INN AURELIA, ITALY

Psychic Shonali Thakur has very firm ideas about what makes for a haunted place. She dismisses the idea that haunted places can be beautiful.

"Haunted places can't be beautiful or peaceful," she says adamantly. "Sadly, that is something the idealists will tell you, but remember a spirit is someone who is unhappy; they are lingering here, troubled, unable to move on. No haunted place is beautiful, my friend. I wish it was like that.

"A haunted place means whoever lived there or died there didn't have a natural death. If the spirits have left unfinished business it could be anything from a loved one left grieving, sickness, or somebody who harmed them in some way. There are many things to keep a spirit grounded to the earth – they're just not ready or able to move into the light."

For Shonali, the haunted place she can't get out of her mind is the Holiday Inn Aurelia in Rome. The popular hotel in the heart of the Eternal City was frequented by the flight crews from Air India airlines for whom Shonali worked as a flight attendant for several years.

"This hotel is extremely haunted," Shonali says. "In the Roman era there was a lot of torture; just look at what they did to the Christians. They had very cruel games. The Coliseum is said to be very haunted, just look at the countless Christians who were thrown to the Lions among other horrors. They had a lot of fun dreaming up ways to be mean and cruel to people.

"All of that horror has remained. If you are torturing human beings, that is not a good way to die. Wherever human beings have been tortured to death, that place is certainly going to be haunted. Anybody who has had an unnatural death, there is going to be a haunting where they dwelled."

Shonali believes her encounter with a troubled and violent spirit in the Holiday Inn was a result of that hotel not cleansing the premises of old spirits.

"The Indians believe in removing the old Shamins (spirits), but a lot of countries don't believe in doing that.

"A lot of people don't believe in cleansing ceremonies to remove spirits that are known to be haunting places. They would rather just cover it up and lock the room, not use the place rather than performing the cleansing required to relieve and release the spirits."

Shonali believes it was the lack of "cleansing" that led to her horrific encounter with a troubled soul at the Rome hotel.

"The room number was 200," she recalls. "It was an old room, and all the crew I worked with had stories with which to regale me. Some who stayed in Room 200 woke to find scratch marks on their backs, some just didn't sleep, tormented with fear. There were all kinds of stories coming out.

"So this day we arrived and I wanted a connecting room to be close to my workmates. The only connecting room available was Room 200 and I opted to take it. People tried to put me off and the receptionist also agreed to change the room. Normally they don't change rooms for flight crews. She seemed very amiable. 'If you don't want to stay there you can stay in another room,' she assured me.

"I was a bit bold at the time. I thought my spiritual practice was strong. I told my friends, 'I refuse to be haunted. The ghosts should be scared of me.' That was my response."

But the moment Shonali entered the musty room she knew there was a presence.

"It was around 4:30 in the afternoon," she recalls. "The thing I noticed immediately upon entering the room – I saw something white go past the mirror. It was like a cloudy figure.

"I thought maybe I was imagining it, so I didn't dwell on it and went to dinner with my friends.

"That night when I slept I had a very, very strange dream. The dream was a about a family travelling. There was a lady in a ball gown wearing long black gloves that went up to her elbows. And there was a man in a tuxedo. They were in a wooden carriage with wooden wheels driven by four to six horses and it was on a climb up a hill.

"One of the wooden wheels seemed to veer off the road while turning and it flipped and the woman kept screaming, 'Save me, save me.' The desperate man tried to save her by trying to pull her back up onto the wagon. But while pulling her up, her gloves slipped off her arm and from her hand and he was left holding only her gloves while she slipped away over a cliff. I heard her screaming as she fell to her death. I saw her falling, then I woke up."

Shonali dismissed it as "just a strange dream."

"I remember thinking, 'what an odd dream to have in a hotel,'" she recalls. "The next morning we did our usual rounds of going to Saint Peters and sightseeing. Before we knew it, it was Siesta time (between 2 and 4pm) so we headed back to our hotel and said we'd have a bit of a lie in and regroup later on in the evening.

"As soon as I entered my room, I saw a pair of long black gloves lying in front of the bed. I didn't think of the lady with the long black gloves who had come to me in my dream. I called housekeeping and said, 'I think you have left something behind in my room.' The housekeeper was insistent she hadn't. 'No, no, no, they are not my gloves,' she said. 'We don't wear those kind of gloves.'"

Shonali decided she would put the mystery of the black gloves to the back of her mind and enjoy a peaceful Siesta.

"I went to lie down on the bed to have a little rest," she says. "I lay down on the bed; I normally sleep on my side. I suddenly felt the bed dip like when somebody else sits on the bed. I felt this huge dip in the bed, but before I could even say anything or think anything, I felt somebody sit on me. They were sitting on me side saddle. I was totally awake, not dreaming and totally terrified. For some reason, I couldn't call out.

"The thing that I should not have done, but I did, was turn on my back. So this 'thing' sat on my chest, it was sitting down on my chest the heaviest and darkest of weights. I felt my throat muscles stretch and the 'thing' entered me.

"Whatever entity it was, I felt it very strongly inside me, I knew at that point that I was no longer the same person. I could feel everything felt different, even though I looked the same. Unless you have had a possession, you cannot imagine how it feels.

"I remember my Grandmother telling me the spirits only enter when you are weak and you have to fight them mentally. You can't give in, you have to say, 'This is my temple and you have to leave.'

"All I could hear was this maniacal laugh in the background of my brain saying, 'I'm not going to go and there is nothing you can do.' At that point I tried to scream really loud, but no sound came out. I was really screaming.

"I tried to reach for my phone but couldn't reach it. I tried to say my Indian prayers, but the voice came out really weird. Then suddenly – and I don't know what made me say it – but I said, 'Jesus save me'. The moment I managed to utter those words, the wooden venetian blinds in the window, which were very heavy, crashed to the ground and the entity that possessed me was gone.

"I was completely drained, emotionally and physically. I crawled to my friend's room; I was on the floor when she found me. I had not a shred of energy. I could not stand.

"The moment my friends saw me they knew straight away and they chorused. 'We told you not to go in there!' I didn't tell them the whole experience, because people who do not believe in possession would not understand."

Was there a connection between the spirit that possessed her, the haunting dream of the falling lady and the mysterious black gloves that appeared in her room?

"To this day, I just don't know," Shonali, 50, says, shaking her head. "It is hard to say. I think the gloves and the lady are separate from the entity that took me over. The fact is in that room there is a spirit now, whether it is the spirit of the lady… I don't know. I didn't go in to detail in following up on the falling lady. But the gloves that appeared in my room were identical to the gloves she wore in my dream.

"I can't explain what happened, but I have no doubt the room was haunted."

Shonali, who has had a psychic gift since childhood, has had many encounters with ghosts. She says ghosts and hotels often go hand in hand.

Shonali checked in to the Taj Mahal Palace Hotel in Mumbai when it reopened in 2010. The historic hotel had been the target for an evil terrorist attack in November 2008 which saw 166 people murdered and more than 300 wounded.

"I can communicate with ghosts," she says. "If they want to show themselves to me I can sometimes see them. I mainly see their energy and their movement. I mainly hear them.

"Visiting the newly opened Taj Mahal Palace Hotel in Mumbai was truly frightening. Before I entered, I had prepared myself. As soon as I entered, I could hear the screaming, I started fretting and my heart rate went up.

"I turned to my friend and said, 'You have to get me out of here'. So we ran out. I was shaking uncontrollably. There was a terrible energy in there.

"I said to my friend, 'They haven't done a good job with the cleansing.' I could literally hear the people screaming and I had flashes of what went on inside the hotel and it was not good. They have since done another cleansing, and it is better.

"I can't stress enough the importance of protecting yourself when you enter haunted places. "You need to pray for protection, you need to have someone with you who knows about white light energy. You need to protect yourself.

"To anyone who thinks it's a game and fun to muck around with the paranormal: beware. It's most certainly not a game and it's not fun. Things can go really wrong and it can be highly dangerous. As I said, there is no such thing as a beautiful haunted place."

* * *

HOTEL CHELSEA, UNITED STATES

They say it has more ghosts than guests. A hotel so quirky, so brilliantly bohemian, that it was more than a hotel – it has been home to some of the most famous writers, musicians, artists and actors the world has seen.

Looming large and darkly moody, with its trademark cast-iron balconies, weather-beaten red bricks and grand staircase that sweeps up and up and up over 12 floors, the Hotel Chelsea, its architecture a schizophrenic mix of Queen Anne Revival and Victorian Gothic, looked haunted way before the ghosts even came calling.

Punk Legend Sid Vicious of The Sex Pistols and former longtime resident and one of the key players in the Chelsea's infamy, once said of the Hotel, "It's a vortex – an artistic tornado of death and destruction and love and broken dreams."

Another deeply talented and troubled soul, Janis Joplin, summed it up best with, "A lot of funky things happen in the Chelsea." Many suggest she wasn't just referring to the seedy, rock'n'roll way of life that was carried out freely and unhindered within the Chelsea's walls, but rather the spine tingling, unexplained paranormal events that happen there on a daily basis.

From the day it opened its now creaking doors in 1884, the Chelsea was a magnet for the creatively gifted and tortured. No royalty has deemed to visit, but kings and queens of talent and artistic endeavor have all enjoyed happy reigns there.

Bob Dylan, Madonna, Quentin Crisp, Jimi Hendrix, Arthur Miller, Andy Warhol, Jack Kerouac, Leonard Cohen and Dylan Thomas are just some of the few who held court at the Chelsea and some stayed on to haunt it.

In 1978, at the height of the Punk Rock era, Sex Pistols guitarist

Sid Vicious moved in to Room 100 with his daffy girlfriend, Nancy Spungen.

Sid and Nancy, as the film of the same name would later show, had a violent, volatile and destructive relationship. They lived out their lives at the Chelsea in a blur of heavy drug taking.

It was in the late hours of October 12 or the early hours of the 13th, a loud cry was heard coming from Room 100. The cry went unheeded as the residents chose to ignore it, "Just Sid and Nancy at it again, always rowing then making up with loud, stupid sex," a former Chelsea resident remembers. "Then all hell broke loose."

The next morning, Sid made a call to the front desk requesting assistance to Room 100. When staff came calling they found the grisly sight of Nancy stabbed to death in the blood-drenched bathroom.

An incoherent Sid, undeniably smashed and crying uncontrollably, was arrested for her murder. He was marched from the Chelsea in a drug-addled haze. He confessed to the murder, but later retracted it.

Whilst out on bail, a lonely and broken man without his beloved Nancy, Sid Vicious died of a heroin overdose – the drugs procured for him by his mother – in Greenwich Village. February 2, 1979. He was just 21.

From the moment of his tragic death, strange goings on have been consistently reported from Room 100. Most people who have dared to stay in the room have endured paranormal experiences.

These reports range from orbs, extreme temperature fluctuations, and particularly disturbingly, the yells and anger of a couple fighting when there is clearly no one else but the guests in the room. Interestingly, it is the ghost of Sid Vicious and not the ghost of Nancy that seems to have the strongest presence.

The ghost of Sid Vicious has been seen in the elevator. Visitors swear they have seen him opening and closing the doors and operating the buttons.

As if the paranormal theories aren't spine-tingling enough, another bizarre claim has Sid Vicious a-la Dr Who, using Room 100 as a portal for travel between two worlds. He comes back to life from the spirit world fruitlessly searching for Nancy. When he doesn't find her, he returns broken and tormented to the spirit world via Room 100.

While Sid is said to come and go, there is another ghost, Mary, who is said to be the most witnessed apparition at The Chelsea. Mary survived the sinking of the Titanic, but sadly, her husband, like so many men, perished and bravely went down with the ill-fated White Star Liner.

An inconsolable Mary checked in to the Chelsea to find solace and sadly was never able to check out. Driven to insanity by her grief, Mary was reported to have hung herself in her room.

Since her tragic passing, many guests at the hotel have witnessed a sad and forlorn lady staring at her reflection in the mirror. Mary is said to be fastidious to a fault, preening herself for hours and admiring her reflection, waiting for a man who won't be showing – her husband lost at sea at rest with the debris of the Titanic one of many corpses on the floor of the Atlantic Ocean.

Mary is said to become highly nervy and agitated if she realizes she is being observed during her prolonged grooming episodes.

Emmy Award-winning actor, Michael Imperioli, swears he encountered Mary's ghost on the 8th floor of The Chelsea. Best known for his role as Christopher Moltisanti on The Sopranos, Imperioli was returning to his hotel room late one night. He saw a woman sobbing whilst looking at herself in a hall mirror. The kind-hearted Imperioli approached her to ask if she was okay, but as he drew near, she vanished before his startled eyes.

Welsh poet Dylan Thomas also resided at The Chelsea in Room 206.

He arrived at the New York landmark located at 222 West 23rd Street, Chelsea, Manhattan with a raft of serious health issues – chief among these a serious love of drinking.

He was in town promoting his latest masterpiece, Under Milkwood, when his health took a bad turn. New York smog was at its worst and did not help Thomas, who suffered severe respiratory problems. The fact that he'd been out on a bender at his beloved White Horse pub also didn't do the gifted poet any favors.

He'd returned to the Chelsea that night declaring, "I've just had 18 straight whiskies. I think that's the record." He was taken from the Chelsea that night in an ambulance. Some blamed quack doctors who sustained Thomas with large doses of morphine for his death.

He died on the 9th of November, 1953. The cause of his death was listed as pneumonia, brain swelling and fatty liver. Moments after his death, Thomas was seen lurking around Room 206. He has been regularly spotted near this room ever since, despite being taken back to Wales where he was buried.

The troubled poet is said to appear as a disembodied head. He has been seen hovering at the end of beds aglow in darkened rooms, quietly watching those who are asleep.

Eerily, it is as if Dylan Thomas is playing out the words of his now seemingly prophetic poems, "Do not go gentle into that good night" and "Death shall have no dominion."

At the time of writing, the hotel was undergoing a controversial renovation during which the resident ghosts were said to be having a field day.

So many people have died at the Chelsea and so many died tragically and young. This has been cited as the main reason why the Chelsea is such a hotbed for paranormal activity.

Renovations are said to particularly stir up spirits not yet at rest.

Since the renovation alone, ghostly encounters have intensified. Among the documented and recorded phenomena are full body apparitions, the sounds of violent arguments, sobbing, orbs, disembodied limbs, and feelings of being touched or stroked.

The most common report has been a sense of foreboding when entering the premises. People describe this as a "black cloud" suddenly descending upon them.

And when the hotel re-opens, it may have a shiny new lick of paint, and some fresh-faced new occupants, but the ghosts will always linger. And so too the ever-descending black cloud of New York's iconic Chelsea Hotel.

❖ The Algonquin is still playing host to Doroty Parker and her pals ❖

Another iconic New York hotel to undergo a renovation is the legendary Algonquin. Built in 1902, The Algonquin is New York City's oldest continuously working hotel.

And like The Chelsea, here was another hotel that played host to all sorts of literati glitterati. It was within these hallowed rooms the legend of the "Long Lunch" was born. Here in moody light, amid the glinting of polished cutlery and booze-laden glasses and sumptuous lounges, the Round Tablers would meet for lunch. They were a group of writers, actors, critics, editors – a clutch of creatives all hell-bent of generating riveting and witty discussion.

Chief among the Round Table group was the sharp of mind, quick-witted Dorothy Parker. Famously asked to put horticulture into a sentence, she quipped straight away, "You can lead a whore to culture, but you can't make her think."

Such remarks as these were quickly spread around New York and the world and The Round Table became celebrated in the 1920s for its members' lively, witty conversation and urbane sophistication. Sometimes their wit was so acerbic the group became known as "The Vicious Circle."

Apart from Parker, New Yorker founder Harold Ross, Harpo Marx, actor and writer Robert Benchley were also among those who made their way through New York's streets to lunch at the Round Table in the Dining Room of the Algonquin.

But perhaps the long lunch of the Round Tablers has run a little long with reports that Dorothy Parker and her pals are still haunting the dining room.

Their clinking cutlery and chinking crystal High Ball glasses have become louder since the Algonquin underwent a renovation in 2004. Paranormal researchers will quickly tell you the easiest way to summon a ghost is to do a renovation. Ghosts detest change and loathe structural changes.

Since the Algonquin's reno, Dorothy Parker's ghost has been seen getting out of an elevator and heading to the dining room. Strange noises have been heard, laughter ringing out and the sound of lively chatter when the lights to the Dining Room have been turned out. There is little doubt the Vicious Circle is back holding court in what may be the world's longest and most haunted lunch.

* * *

THE HYDRO MAJESTIC, AUSTRALIA

Staring Paintings, Floating Heads and Haunted,

Forbidden Bedrooms

Glowing whiter than a ghost, this grand dame of Australian hotels sits atop a lofty ridge - the crowning glory to the breathtaking majesty of Australia's Blue Mountains.

The Hydro Majestic at Medlow Bath was the brainchild of Mark Foy, the visionary retail magnate and then owner of Australia's largest Department Store, Mark Foys.

Well-travelled and wealthy, Mark had long wanted to open a grand hotel offering "water cures", the likes of which he'd encountered on his many tours of hotels throughout Europe.

Scouring the Blue Mountains for a spectacular location, he purchased three adjacent properties at Medlow, the second highest point in the vast mountain range. The properties, perched precariously on a cliff-top, offered unhindered views to the sprawling Megalong Valley below.

There were three separate buildings on each of the properties, and Mark Foy, using the most modern of Architectural techniques available at the time, managed to join the buildings all together with a series of long glass walled galleries, richly carpeted and filled with natural light. Many critics at the time disparagingly said the buildings looked like they had been sticky taped together.

Despite the critics, the Hydro opened with a lavish weekend on the 4th of July 1904. The who's who of society met for champagne cocktails at Penrith Station located at the foot of the Mountains. They were then ferried by some of the first cars to be seen in Australia – a fleet of De Dion Bouton autos imported by Foy specifically for this grand occasion. It took the VIPs nine hours to reach the lofty perch of the Hydro Majestic. These days, it takes a leisurely hour to get there from Penrith.

In the lead up to the opening, Mark Foy had managed to have the town of Medlow's name changed to Medlow Bath, echoing the treatments on offer at his sumptuous hotel. But on the day of opening, the VIPs were treated to more than a bath – they found themselves engulfed in the biggest snow storm ever recorded in the Blue Mountains.

For years the Hydro was the home away from home for the famous and well-heeled. Dame Nellie Melba, renowned for her seemingly endless "come back" performances, was forever coming back to the Hydro.

Australia's first Prime Minister, Sir Edmund Barton, was a guest at the hotel when he suddenly died there of heart failure on 7 January 1920.

The years saw the Hydro become a faded rose. Ramshackle and rundown, she enjoyed different personas including her being taken over by the US Army and transformed into a military hospital during the course of World War II.

After the war, she returned to being a hotel and stayed in the Foy Family until 1984. She fell into the hands of various people and organizations but with each year she became more run down, her once grand opulence patched up and now dowdy and threadbare.

And of course, with the closing of each decade and further disrepair, the hotel became the place where the dead checked in.

"With that sort of history, of course the place is haunted," says an incredulous former guest, Bethany Burgess, who checked into the hotel with her mother, Laura, for a few days' escape.

"The moment we checked in, we were told to be on the alert for ghosts," Bethany recalls. "The Concierge happily informed us that the resident ghost (as it turned out there is more than one) was living in Room 402 on the next floor above our room. She looked at me with a smile and said, 'Do you mind that?'

"I thought that was a strange thing to ask. You'd think a hotel would be covering up any ghosts so as not to frighten off guests.

I shook my head while trying to clear the lump in my throat and replied with fake nonchalance, 'Of course not, as long as they stay upstairs and don't pay us any visits.'

"A few days into our visit, we were relaxed and high on clean mountain air. We were coming back from dinner and Mum didn't stop at our floor, but kept going up the stairs to the next level.

"'Mum, what are you doing?' I called. She kept walking without replying. It was as if she was in some sort of trance. 'Mum, mum, come back now please,' I yelled, but she kept walking up the stairs. I tried to follow her up the stairs but there was this force – it felt like an invisible wall which prevented me from going further.

"I managed to force my way through. I was determined to get to her and stop whatever it was she was about to do.

"I called to her from the top of the stairs but she kept walking determinedly down the corridor, stopping outside of Room 402.

"She had marched brazenly to the door and, using her knuckles with vigor, knocked loudly. It was a very firm and determined knock.

"She walked back towards me, smiling, and I just shook my head and said, 'Mum, why on earth did you do that for?' She just laughed and said, 'You'll see.'

"That night in bed, I had the most troubled and disturbed sleep. I felt really, really bothered and quite set upon. I woke up and knew that I was being harassed by this ghost. 'Tormented' would be a better way of putting it. It felt like when I was a kid being pummeled by my elder brother who keeps on tormenting you even when you ask him to stop.

"This ghost was on top of me. It was horrible and I kept saying, 'Get off me.'

"In the end I was cranky and exhausted and I thought, 'This is ridiculous.' I remember praying 'Dear Lord, please help get this off me and the moment I prayed it went off me and over to Mum.

"I got out of bed and went to wake mum up. Mum was there moaning and moaning and never did this in her sleep. I went to her and woke her up. I was a bit cranky with her.

"I said, 'Look, you have brought this ghost in here by going and knocking on the door and annoying it. Now it's come and annoyed me and now it's doing it to you. You are going to have to pray. You are going to have to pray that it goes away and you have to ask God's forgiveness that you went and knocked on the door. You thought it was funny – well it clearly isn't.

"Mum was so cute, she prayed like a little girl, using the old-fashioned language she always resorted to when praying. When she finished praying there was a complete calmness in the room. We felt peaceful; we knew the ghost had gone. Exhausted, we were able to sleep. I have no doubt at all the so-called resident ghost had paid us a visit.

"The next morning, I chastised my mother with the words from an old Marilyn Monroe movie. 'In future, Mum,' I said, sternly, 'don't bother to knock.'

But Bethany's encounter with the Hydro's ghostly guests would only intensify.

"Having been kept up most of the night, I was tired the next day," she explains. "I left mum enjoying afternoon tea on the terrace and I went back to the room for an afternoon nap.

"Instead of a restful sleep, I endured a shocking nightmare. I could hear voices circling above my bed. It was a multitude of voices all chattering at once, but I couldn't make out what they were saying.

"They weren't happy voices, and there was an urgency to what they were saying. Try as I might, I couldn't make out what they were saying as there were too many of them, all talking over each other.

"Suddenly, a face came towards me from the left hand side of the bed – not a whole face, just eyes, nose and a mouth and a bit of the top of a head. The face lunged at me and gave me a kiss on the cheek and I screamed."

Bethany rushed from the room and told the woman at the desk of her most recent ghostly encounter.

"Oh, you got The Womaniser up there with you too!" the concierge responded with a knowing smile.

The concierge told Bethany that during the construction of the Hydro there had been a builder nicknamed 'The Womaniser." The builder had murdered his wife and buried her in the foundations of the Hydro Majestic while it was being built.

"He bumped off his wife and kept right on with his philandering ways," the concierge said.

Years later, Bethany returned to the hotel a married woman.

"I thought my encounters with ghosts were long over," she laughs with a shiver. "My then husband and I were sitting by this beautiful, huge fireplace. Above the mantel, there was this massive painting of The Three Sisters at Katoomba.

"I'm a painter, so I was instantly drawn to this grand landscape. The first thing I noticed, there was no signature on the painting to tell me who the artist was. I had noticed on many of the paintings that hung in the Hydro, the artist had remained anonymous.

"'That's strange,' I thought, gazing up at the painting of the Three Sisters. "As I looked into the painting, I started seeing ghosts lurking among the trees. At first they were hidden, but the more I looked, the clearer they would become. Their faces were ghoulish, their expressions sneering and evil.

"There was a large painting in a gold frame of Napoleon on a horse. It still hangs there today in the place they call Cat's Alley. You pass it on your way to the Dining Room. They call it Cat's Alley because the women in their refinery would sit there while the men retired to their Smoking Room to play pool and drink brandy after dinner. The women would sit in this corridor and make catty remarks about other women who promenaded by. 'Oh, look at what she's wearing, how hideous.' That sort of thing."

Bethany found herself falling under the spell of Napoleon's fixed gaze.

"I was looking at the painting and I couldn't help but feel he was eyeing me off," she laughs good-naturedly. "It was as if he was flirting and giving me the come on!

"You know when you walk around and the painting seems to follow you with their eyes – like the Mona Lisa? Napoleon was doing that. Even more chilling, his facial expression kept changing. I remember thinking, 'This is really weird. I'm not imagining this. This painting is giving me the come on and it's really creeping me out.'

"To be truthful, he was a really good looking guy.

"I'd walk away from it and then come back and the painting would look completely different. The expression would have changed again and then it would go back to being a normal painting. I thought, this is too weird."

Bethany fled the determined gaze of Napoleon and sought out the concierge to find out more about the paintings.

"The concierge knew exactly what I was talking about when I brought up Napoleon. 'The cleaner never wants to look at that painting,' she told me. 'She gets the horrors every time she has to go and dust it. She simply says it is evil and she doesn't like it.'"

Bethany says several of the artworks gave her that feeling as well.

"They were really good paintings, but they were definitely haunted, I'd say demonic. The Mountains are teeming with witches and it's as if they have cast their spells and rituals into the paintings.

"We had taken lots of photos of the paintings. When we returned home there was one night, shortly after, my husband woke up in the middle of the night, sweating.

"He'd been having nightmares about the paintings. He turned to me white faced and said, 'We have to cut up the photos we took of the paintings and we have to destroy the negatives.

"I fully agreed. It was as if those paintings were haunting us, hanging on our walls with their force now destroying our house. That night we got out of bed and prayed, then set about destroying any memory of those dreadful demonic paintings."

Years on, Bethany still gets chills recalling her visits to the Hydro Majestic.

"I can't go back there," she says. "I never will. I only have to close my eyes and I can still see those paintings, especially the eyes of Napoleon compelling me to come to him.

"All I know is those experiences were real and too consistent with other reports for me not to believe they actually happened. It wasn't my over-active imagination or my eyes playing tricks on me.

"Those trips to the Hydro and the horrors that came with them make me know I never want to go on any of those ghost tours you hear about. I don't want to invite any of that stuff in. After what I experienced I have no doubt there is stuff happening – there is a world we cannot see; there is a spiritual world. It's dark and demonic. And you shouldn't play around with it. Not that I did. It played around with me."

JULIAN'S VICTORIAN STORY, AUSTRALIA

My Boyfriend Was Murdered. He Told me From the Grave.

Acclaimed Australian hair and makeup artist, Julian Jones, knows what it's like to inhabit a haunted place, for Julian has had his life finely tuned to the world of the paranormal since a very young age.

Intuitive, fun-loving yet fiercely protective of the dead who have not managed to pass on – Julian's supernatural gift is never far from being triggered.

"I initially hear noises, I definitely feel something," Julian says of his communing with ghosts. "It's like there's a train arriving. You know it's coming, you can feel it, you can hear it.

"Sometimes it can be an awkward silence, but that silence brings with it the promise that something supernatural is about to happen. Like I said with the train, you can feel it coming, and you are left waiting with great anticipation."

Julian admits to feeling a bundle of confusion and fear when he feels the dead are first trying to reach him.

"I get a feeling on my skin – that weird feeling that people say is your skin crawling. My hair, just like all the clichés used in scary movies, does stand up. I get this overriding feeling that someone is there, but I often can't see them at first.

"Sometimes it can be as simple as hearing their clothing rustle.

"It really is that analogy of waiting for the train to come, and for me, when it does, it's like being hit with the full force of a freight train. When it hits, it's an engulfing moment."

Julian's most recent 'visitation' involved his former partner making contact with him.

"My ex-partner, who I hadn't seen in over four years, just popped into my head," Julian recalls. "For some reason I picked up the phone to ring him, I just felt this sudden urge to make contact with him. So I looked at my phone and I thought, 'Mmmm, should I or shouldn't I? No I probably shouldn't.' So I put the phone down then picked it up again and thought, 'Come on, just ring him and make sure he's okay.' Then I put the phone down again, then I thought I should ring his mum. I thought, 'Why am I doing this? This guy is in my past.' I didn't ring his mother either. I just tried to put the whole thing out of my head."

But Julian's ex-partner had other ideas.

"That afternoon, I went downstairs to paint my laundry walls. I had chosen white. So I'm in the laundry, painting away when I see my ex appear on the wall, standing there from his chest up and just looking straight into my eyes. His apparition was so clear, but he was still part of the wall. It was like someone was shooting a high definition version of him onto my gleaming white wall. He was literally a paintbrush away from me.

"I was in total shock. I kind of tripped out a bit, all the while thinking, 'Why am I seeing him? Why has he come back into my mind after all this time?' The look in his eyes was so intense, I can't begin to tell you.

"I could physically see him, yet he was slightly transparent. It was one of the clearest apparitions I have seen in my life. I imagine that's because of the connection we had while we were together."

A baffled and stunned Julian quickly put his paintbrushes down and went back upstairs to clear his head.

"I just thought I needed a bit of a break to clear him out of my mind," Julian says. "I spent about five minutes having a cup of tea then thought, 'Right, I'm going to finish these walls no matter what.'

"So I returned to my laundry walls and there he was again. He looked the same but this time his eyes were more intense, staring at me as if to say, 'Take note of what you are seeing.' I was like 'Aaaaaaagh!' Freaked out and frustrated. I washed my brushes, put them away, and that was it."

The next morning, Julian's phone rang at around 6:15am.

"It was a Monday morning, and I receive this call from one of my friends who was working at the ABC studios in the makeup room. She said, 'Jules, I think your ex-partner might be a missing person.

He was a computer expert wasn't he?' And I'm like, 'Yes.'

"She said, 'I'm pretty sure it's him. Turn on the news now because they are going to do an update on him.' So I turned on the ABC news and sure enough, there he was.

"I was gutted – floored – and I tripped out a bit because of what I'd seen on the wall in my laundry."

Julian's ex had left his mother's house on the 9th of October 2014. The last sighting of him was on the 10th of October.

"And he appeared to me in the laundry on the 11th," Julian says. "Sadly, there has been no outcome. We assumed that he has been murdered. They found his car on Picton Road in NSW and he's from Victoria."

Julian believes his ex-partner has been murdered.

"I think he appeared to me because he was trying to tell me, 'This is really serious, I'm in deep trouble," he says. "I then started getting visions of him being hit over the head. I believe I was seeing him being murdered.

"Where they found his car is of no significance. I have a feeling he has gone on a blind date that's gone wrong. He certainly wasn't the suicidal type when I knew him. He certainly wasn't a visitor to gay beats; he was against all that type of stuff. He was just a very gentle, really, really sweet, really funny, quite caring man."

Julian says he's haunted by his ex-partner's pleading eyes.

"Seeing his eyes freaked me out the most. When you've been intimate with someone, you know their eyes pretty well. The visions I had of him – there was trouble in his eyes. He was in trouble."

Julian's mother, Annie, who can hear the voices of the deceased, came to spend time with her shaken son. Julian says he gets his psychic gift from his mum.

"As mum stayed with me, the one thing we kept coming back to was the question if Atilla was dead or alive," Julian says. "Mum was sleeping at my country home in rural Victoria and I was preparing for bed in my bedroom.

"I sat down on my mattress and I swear I heard my ex say, 'Jules, I'm dead.'

"I thought, 'No, it must be the springs in the mattress, so I sat up and down on the mattress and the springs did not sound like that voice. I thought maybe it was mum calling out, 'Jules, I'm in bed.' And then I heard the voice call again, 'Jules, I'm dead.' It was his voice. I quickly called out, 'Mum, did you just say something?' Mum stumbled out of bed, rubbing her eyes and scratching her head. 'Love, I was asleep, what did you say?' she replied. I asked her if she had just called out to me telling me she was in bed. 'No I didn't say anything, I was fast asleep,' she replied.

"I slumped back on my bed, knowing my ears hadn't been playing tricks on me. 'I was just hoping you had said something so I wouldn't have to face up to the fact I clearly heard Atilla tell me, "Jules, I'm dead."'

"Mum's jaw dropped. And she knew. It was then and there we had to accept: Atilla was dead and he was calling out to me. As long as his disappearance remains unsolved, he will probably keep coming to me."

Julian is no stranger to having the dead reach out to him from beyond the grave.

He remembers the first time he had a particularly heartfelt encounter with an apparition at his family home in Glen Waverly, Victoria, in 1975.

"I was very young, I was six," Julian recalls. "My sister, Leyvette, five, who had many health issues as a youngster had just passed away. She was a beautiful girl, but sadly had spent most of her young life basically living at the Children's Hospital.

"My brother Marcus and I had been put to bed and all our family were gathered in the lounge room crying over the death of our sister. We could hear them crying so brokenly. It was hard to listen to. So my brother and I hopped into bed together and we huddled together listening to the cries of our relatives down the hallway.

"The next thing you know, our sister's standing in the doorway of our bedroom and she was wearing one of her outfits she liked to get around in. It wasn't hospital clothing, it was one of her white-and blue-striped dresses that she loved.

"As plain as day, she was standing there and said, 'Hello Marky (her name for Marcus), hello Ju Ju (her name for me) 'Can I hop into bed with you?'

"We said 'Yes,' and we pulled back our covers and she climbed in with us. We knew our relatives were crying about her death down the hallway and here we were, my brother and I cuddled up in bed with her.

"That was a very surreal and precious moment, and my brother and I still remember it like it was yesterday and often talk about it today."

Jules says he never saw his sister again after that.

"We didn't make a fuss about it the next morning as I knew my father wasn't a believer," he says. "My sister did visit again when I was 16 or 17, but I didn't see her, Mum did.

"I recall I was sitting in the lounge room when I saw a white figure come through the front door and go across the hallway into our spare room.

"Mum came home shortly after and I told her what I'd seen. 'Perhaps it was your sister,' she soothed.

"I went to wash the dishes and shortly after, Mum came into the kitchen. 'Oh my God,' she exclaimed hoarsely and sounding shocked. 'Your sister is standing right behind you and she's holding her arms out to you.'

"I couldn't see her, but I just put my hand out to her and welcomed her, which I normally wouldn't do to any spirits but this was my sister. Mum said she could see Leyvette reaching her hand out to mine, but I didn't touch her. But it was a beautiful haunting moment."

As a child, Julian – much to the vexation of his concerned father – had several encounters with ghosts.

"I kept hearing groaning voices next to my head," he remembers. "I'd be in my bedroom and I'd hear groans and moans. And this was a new-built house so there shouldn't have been any spirits there.

"They were sinister voices and when I asked my father and brother one morning could they hear the voices, they just smiled good-naturedly and looked at me as if I was a bit of a whack job."

Julian was taken to see a leading child psychologist, who listened to his stories of hearing the voices of the dead. He concluded Julian, was "A very mature young man with no mental issues whatsoever."

"But after seeing my sister, things progressed," he confesses. "I was a bit naughty and I had a few poltergeist experiences as a teenager. Unbeknownst to me, I had conjured them up myself by performing séances. I just thought it was a bit of fun.

"I got together with some friends and we tried to conjure the spirit of a young child who had recently drowned in my friend's backyard pool. We were actually gathered at my friend's place in Templestow, Victoria where the tragic drowning had occurred.

"We really were just inquisitive teenagers and we wanted to talk to this poor little boy to see if he was okay. We got more than we bargained for.

"We set up a Ouija board we'd made ourselves and the glass we were using to guide us to the letters suddenly rose up off the table. Terrified, I remember staring up at my friend's mother who was standing at the kitchen bench making us lunch. Her eyes were literally popping out of her head. She looked at me and then at the glass, with her eyes bursting out of her head. Then she screamed, and said, 'You stop this right now!'

"We were all so shocked and frightened. We quickly scooped up the letters and burned them. We thought this would make things stop.

"Suddenly this big, heavy sliding door that ran between the backyard pool and kitchen/dining room came flying off its runners, flew up in to the air about six feet, then smashed down on the dining room table. There was no wind, nothing, to cause the door to do that. All of us were screaming and running for our lives. My friend's mother looked like she was about to have a stroke. None of us had ever been so frightened. I ran up the hallway to my friend's bedroom with him following close behind.

"Out of nowhere, this five cent coin comes flying by our heads. It hits a radio cassette player and music started playing. I don't think I've ever weed myself so easily in my life.

"I kept thinking, what have I done? I was in big trouble and I was blamed for the whole thing.

"My mum was so angry with me. 'You're not to have séances anymore,' she snapped in the car on the drive home. 'You are banned from having them ever.'

"I learned a big lesson that day: not to play around with stuff like that. We were treating it like a game; a scary but fun adventure.

We didn't see we weren't protecting ourselves, that we were leaving ourselves open to all kinds of dark evil because we didn't cover ourselves with prayer or white light.

"I want to tell young people reading this book, the spirit world is alive and real, just as real as you and I living and breathing. I advise you not to play around with it. I'd stay out of graveyards and old abandoned buildings, because you just might conjure something you really shouldn't and don't need to. If you have to do that sort of thing, you really must take with you someone who is wise in this area, someone older and able to cover you in white light and say prayers to protect you."

Despite his sage advice, Julian just can't seem to stay away from the world he warns us against.

"My trouble is I have this super sensitive gift and the spirits seek me out.

"They can appear anytime, anywhere. You could be walking along a quiet road, or in my case, just doing something ordinary like painting a laundry wall.

"Although it's spooky, scary even – the great unknown usually is – I'm grateful these spirits make themselves known. Sometimes it can be as innocent as a great grandparent coming to steal a peek at their great grandchildren. Or it could be a malevolent, if there has been a murder in a house for instance. These spirits tend to repeat the murder, so you might be hearing gunshots or banging if someone has been bashed before they were murdered. You will hear the horrific scene played out again and again.

"Often if somebody who has been a victim of an unsolved crime and the case remains open, that spirit will try to contact you. I think that is what has happened with my missing ex-partner. I just wish he'd make contact again and tell me exactly what happened to him. If they all did this, there'd be a lot of cold cases finally put to rest along with the tormented, lost souls."

* * *

THE KENT SCHOOL SCHWALMTAL – "A SPECIAL ORPHANAGE", GERMANY

It was established as an act of divine Grace and mercy. A place offering compassion and shelter to 600 unwanted mentally handicapped and severely disabled.

Here, along the serene halls of Saint Jozefsheim monastry, run by an order of Franciscan monks, the broken and downcast were made to feel whole and loved again.

It was 1913 and this sprawling collection of buildings comprising a church, a school, living quarters and administration buildings was a beacon of hope, love and charity.

Sadly, with the coming to power of the Nazis, all the goodness that ran through that hallowed place of peace was turned over to evil. The Franciscan monks were persecuted, falsely accused of sex crimes, driven to bankruptcy, murdered and ultimately driven out.

With the rise of Hitler in 1939, the monastery was seized and given the name Wadniel Hostert. The Nazis euphemistically called it a "Special Orphanage" for children who were not welcome in the so-called perfect world of the Third Reich.

The Special Orphanage would be the murderous dumping ground for Jewish and disabled children.

The Nazis made it law that all disabled children must be reported. These children, along with Jewish youngsters, were herded up and transported to these "orphanages", which really were elaborate Killing Centers. The Wadniel Hostert was chief among these hellish centres.

The once beautiful "Guardian Angel House" of the Franciscan Brothers now became the center for murdering innocent children. Their deaths were not quick and clean. They were prolonged and

Saint Jozefsheim monastry, first communion, 1935.

torturous. The children were drugged with Luminal and if they woke up they would be dosed again. The ordeal of dying could drag on sometimes for eight days.

The head Nazi doctor at the Waldniel Hostert was Georg Renno, who has been held responsible for the murder of 28,000 people during the Second World War. In his crazed time at the Waldniel Hostert, he killed 512 young innocent souls. Their death certificates were blatant works of fiction with the cause of deaths being put down to emaciation, pneumonia, cardiovascular weakness and other appalling lies to cover up their cold-blooded murders.

Since the war, the complex has served as a British Military Hospital and then as an educational institution known as the Kent School.

But the stirring memory of those children and their harrowing plight at the sadistic hand of the Nazis was never far from anyone who visited the complex after the war.

"You felt it the moment you entered the buildings," Louise Cassar, who visited the complex in the early 90s, says. "I could sense their bewilderment, their overwhelming terror.

"Imagine suddenly being taken from your parents and placed in such a brutal, cold setting. These were mentally disabled children. Imagine their terror. They would not have known what fate had in store for them, but they would have known this was not a good place."

The building has been for sale for many years now. It is falling into disrepair, and its haunted history is making it next to impossible for the current owner to sell.

It has been widely reported that the former Nazi Institution of Horror is haunted by the ghosts of the mentally disabled children and young adults who were murdered during the evil reign of the Third Reich.

"These were cruelly slain innocents," Louise says. "Little wonder their tormented souls are left to wander the empty corridors and grounds of the complex."

Many have heard the children screaming and weeping. Night fall has seen the most recorded paranormal activity.

Many former students of the school have come forward to say they always sensed something bad had happened there.

"They didn't hide things very well," former student Sam George said on social media. "There was an aura to the place that was very disconcerting at times."

Whether or not the place is sold and transformed into a new creation, those who were murdered there will forever walk its hallways, compelling us never to forget their little lives in history that must not be denied.

* * *

LIZZIE BORDEN'S HOUSE, UNITED STATES

"Lizzie Borden took an axe,
And gave her mother forty whacks.
When she saw what she had done,
She gave her father forty-one."

Playgrounds throughout the Western World have often echoed with schoolgirls reciting this cheery song. The children chant it and chortle as they turn a heaving skipping rope and hapless girls run in and hope their feet will know when to jump at just the right time.

They're so caught up in jumping rope they don't realize they are innocently singing about one of the most grisly axe murders of all time. They think it's just another fun ditty, like Ring A Ring A Rosie – and that lovely nursery rhyme was actually about the plague!

Take away the fun of jumping rope and the song is positively creepy, as is the Legend of Lizzie Borden.

And the eerie Victorian weatherboard house located at 92 Second Street, Fall River, Massachusetts, where the Borden family lived and where Mr. and Mrs. Borden were bludgeoned to death with a hatchet, is now regarded as one of the most haunted places on the planet. That's a pretty big boast. But anyone who has stayed at the house, now called the Lizzie Borden Bed and Breakfast, will back up the grandiose claim.

The Borden home was built in 1845. Two stories high and looking somber, it is painted dark green and its windows bear black shutters. It has an attic and a cellar, all the perfect hallmarks of a haunted house. It was when the Borden family moved in a few years later that the house took on a rather dark aura.

Andrew Borden, a banker, was said to be very tight-minded and miserly. He was wealthy but feared ever losing his wealth. Such was his meanness, he refused to buy fresh food when there was still food in the house. The Borden family often ate spoiled, rotten food.

In the 1975 horror movie, *The Legend Of Lizzie Borden*, starring Elizabeth Montgomery, there is a famous scene where the Borden family sit down to dinner, a stew so rancid it is crawling with maggots. A horrified Lizzie runs outside to be violently ill, while her greedy, tight father and fearful stepmother, Abby, wolf the meal down gleefully.

It is said Andrew Borden ruled the family sternly and was incapable of showing love openly. The family "got along," tiptoeing around him and his moods. He would impose his will on them.

Lizzie and her sister Emma lived miserably within the Borden house. They didn't like their stepmother, even though she had tried to be a mother to them when she married the widower, Andrew, at the age of 36.

The girls had been raised in a rigid, unhappy atmosphere and most of the time they were said to take out their bitterness and unhappiness on poor scapegoat Abby who was equally miserable and felt shackled by her marriage.

Nerves were frayed, the Borden women walked as living ghosts through the rooms of the house, just existing. There were no gentlemen callers for Lizzie and Emma who were now in their 30s. The mean-spirited reputation of their father was widely known – visitors to the Borden home were a scarcity.

It was a hot August 4 morning the day Mr. and Mrs. Borden were murdered. Andrew had gone to his precious bank and Emma was out of town, which left Lizzie, Abby and their maid, Maggie, to tend to household duties.

Maggie was cleaning windows downstairs, and Abby went up to the second floor to straighten things in the guest bedroom. The girl's uncle, John Morse (the brother of their late mother, Sarah) had been one of the rare visitors who had stayed over on the night of the third. He was said to be a rather "odd one, given to peculiar behavior." He had taken his leave.

As Abby went to making the bed, she was crept up on. A hand quickly pulled down the window shade; a startled Abby turned around and was felled with a violent hatchet blow to her forehead.

Slumped on the floor face down, her killer hacked her a further 19 times.

Maggie, meanwhile, had done with her window washing and went up to her room to rest.

Andrew came home from the bank early that day. The heat was getting to him and he said he wasn't feeling well. He had laid down on the couch. His killer had crept up on him from behind. Andrew was hacked to death in a hatchet-wielding frenzy. The attack only stopped after the hatchet handle broke off when the blade became embedded in his skull.

Andrew's face was so pulverized he was unrecognizable. His death photos show one eye cut in half and protruding in a ghastly manner from its socket.

The murders caused an instant scandal. A haphazard police investigation saw Lizzie charged with the murders of her father and stepmother. The press had a field day. The murders were shocking and violent beyond belief – they were allegedly carried out by a rich but deeply unhappy female. Little wonder the trial of Lizzie Borden captured the world's attention.

But there was not enough evidence that Lizzie actually committed the crimes. She was acquitted of the murders. No one else was ever charged with the crimes.

Lizzie and Emma inherited a huge chunk of their rich father's estate, left their house of horrors and bought a new abode. The Borden sisters lived together for 10 years, but life wasn't easy with Lizzie being gossiped about and many of her neighbors pointing the finger and insisting she was a parent murderer.

The sisters fell out in 1905. Nobody knows the real reason why Emma Borden suddenly moved out. It is speculated she may have not been happy with Lizzie's close friendship with another woman, Nance O'Neil. Others claim she found out the truth about the axe murders and fled in disgust. Household staff would not be drawn on the rift.

Lizzie's remaining years were disturbed and reclusive. She died of pneumonia in Fall River, on June 1 1927. Emma died just days later in Newmarket, New Hampshire.

But the legend of Lizzie Borden only intensified with the passing

of years. The 1975 telemovie, starring Elizabeth Montgomery as Lizzie – a million miles removed from her endearing Samantha in the smash-hit comedy series, *Bewitched* – caused an instant sensation and a renewed interest in Lizzie and the Borden axe murders.

The Borden home became a fixation among ghoulish sightseers, television crews and paranormal investigators. And when, in 1996, it became a Bed and Breakfast, customers flocked to stay there and be scared out of their wits by reveling in the home's creepiness.

The furniture in the house is as the Borden's left it. Graphic crime scene photos are prominently displayed, leaving nothing to the imagination. Guests are encouraged to recline on the sofa where Mr. Borden was bludgeoned or lie down on the very spot where Abby was felled. Guests can also pose with a reproduction of the infamous hatchet if they wish.

Fun and games aside, most guests at the Lizzie Borden B & B come away with little doubt the house is haunted.

Some have heard a woman weeping softly at night. Other's claim a piano key is struck – the same note over and over in the dead of night. When people go to see who is making the racket, no one is there.

Shadow people have been seen on the stairs. They say the ghost of Lizzie Borden, tormented by the crime she was accused of, wanders the rooms. Others insist they see her in the cellar as if she is trying to conceal evidence. The rooms where the murders were carried out are rife with supernatural activity as if the crimes are being carried out over and over.

Some have seen the ghost of the maid Maggie. Others swear they have seen the ghost of a cat lurking in the cellar. Before she was killed, Abby Borden had found their cat in the basement with its head hacked off.

There are also the usual reports of flickering lights and orbs and TV crews befuddled by their equipment malfunctioning for no reason.

For those not creeped out enough, the movie starring Elizabeth Montgomery and the creepy theme song are in constant rotation. It's not widely known, but Elizabeth Montgomery and Lizzie Borden were sixth cousins once removed, both descending from 17th-century Massachusetts resident John Luther.

Spookily, many claim the haunting song has also enticed the ghost of Lizzie Borden to come out to play. There is a popular story that around the time of the Lizzie Borden movie, a group of girls were playing with a skipping rope when they were approached by a faded looking lady in unusual period dress.

The lady smiled and had a tear in her eye. She asked if she could have a go at turning the rope. The girls happily obliged. The girls started singing the Lizzie Borden song as they skipped and the woman, staring blankly, became agitated. She started turning the rope in a frenzied, whipping manner. The girls screamed as the force and speed of the spinning rope intensified. One girl's ankles bled as they were lashed by the rope. The song stopped and the woman suddenly vanished. The front door of the Borden house was heard to slam, while the shaken girls were left crying in the gutter.

* * *

MAITLAND GAOL, AUSTRALIA

My Fright Night in a Haunted Gaol

The author was dared by a National Magazine to share a cell with the troubled souls of evil murderers in Australia's notoriously haunted Maitland Gaol.

Behind the sandstone walls of deserted Maitland Gaol, in the famously stunning wine-growing region of the New South Wales Hunter Valley, something sinister stirs.

Here beneath the rolls of razor wire designed to contain some of Australia's most notorious murderers including Ivan Milat (the backpacker murders), and the Anita Cobby killers, lingers a tormenting spirit of foreboding. You can't help but be chilled by a sense of evil.

The dark cells may be empty now – the last prisoners, men who perpetrated some of the country's most violent crimes, were shipped out in 1998 – but even hardened cynics couldn't help but wonder if this historical prison for the violent, demented and deranged is now the lively dwelling place of the dead.

At the time of my chilling visit, I was greeted by psychic guide, Cheryl Newcombe. Cheryl's warm and welcoming smile was soon altered to downcast and fearful as she ushered me through the thundering steel gates that first opened in 1848.

"This is without doubt one of the most haunted places in Australia," she told me. "From the unexplained shadows that appear on the walls to the night that the gates opened and closed by themselves, causing even me to flee.

"Being a psychic, I was embarrassed that I ran out of here. I've never run from a ghost before but I did that night, there was such a sense of evil. But of course there are ghosts here – there is not one cell here that someone hasn't died in. There's a lot of lingering pain here."

It was my assignment to spend a night in this hellhole along with photographer Andrew Jacob. This wasn't some jolly, scream and giggle ghost tour – this was an experiment, to see what two outsiders could feel, indeed see, while being left alone virtually in the dark in this troubled place of evil and sorrows.

We were left to wander the shadowy corridors, rank with the stench of former prisoners, to see if we would have our own close encounter with a ghost. Our shoulders jarred with fear when Cheryl rattled keys and slammed sturdy prison doors loud enough to wake the dead. We can't explain the mysterious lights that flicker in the cells where prisoners hanged themselves before the hooded hangman could reach them.

Cheryl smirked knowingly as she stopped outside a cell with a red paint-chipped door.

"This is your cell," she told me, pulling back the heaving door that weighed more than 80 kilograms. Her torchlight scoured the dank walls before illuminating the scrawl of a past occupant who killed himself in this very room. "Only God Can Judge Me Now," he scribbled across the yellow walls before he hanged himself. I knew at this point I would not be enjoying any pleasant dreams (or any sleep for that matter) while incarcerated for the night inside Maitland Gaol.

"Oh, you won't be sleeping in here alone," Cheryl said, trying to sound reassuring. "Already there are two ghosts settling in next to you. I know they're there because I can clearly see them, and I can see you have gone all cold down your right side. That's their energy to the right of you."

Cheryl was right, I did feel a chill down the right side of my body, and in the fading afternoon light I could feel the place shifting beyond scary.

I remember the unexplained screams that ricocheted off sandstone walls as we entered a deserted exercise yard. Cheryl nodded knowingly.

"Did you hear that?" Andrew and I asked in unison, more than a little disturbed. "What is that screaming?"

"Let's just say it's not the wind," she said, her gaze fixed to the ground. "People report hearing it all the time. It's the screams of some very troubled souls. There was a lot of brutality and sadism committed here. You'll hear the screams in the shower block and the infirmary, too. It's not your imaginations. By the time you've spent your night here, you'll both be emotionally spent."

Strangely, it was Cheryl who suffered as we entered the infirmary.

"I always try to walk through here as best I can," she explained. "I always end up with headaches. You think about the people who died here. I once had the ghost of a woman appear in here telling me to get out as she wanted to go to bed. There were women prisoners here back in the 1800s.

With our heads swimming with sinister tales of murder, torture, and the chilling thought we are in the presence of ghosts, there was no way our overactive imaginations were going to allow for sleep.

The suicide note on the wall of my cell was a constant reminder that troubled souls and death lingered near. There were menacing and mysterious footsteps outside the door and it was only 3am. We were meant to be staying the entire night.

Even the stoic photographer, Andrew, who had entered the gaol a skeptic, complained of a mysterious tingling running through his body.

We didn't last the night and Cheryl awaited us at the front office.

"You've lasted longer than most," she told us, with a cheeky grin. "To be honest, you both look like you've seen a ghost. Funny that!"

To this day, we can't explain what it was exactly, but the Maitland Gaol experience left us with little doubt we had lingered too long in a very haunted place.

To feel what we experienced firsthand, arrange your own tour of the Maitland Gaol.

* * *

THE SEPTEMBER 11 GHOST AT THE FOOT OF THE STAIRS. HAUNTED MANCHESTER, UNITED KINGDOM

Writer John Burfitt was on the trip of a lifetime. He'd just experienced a heady two weeks in New York City, culminating in a breathtaking farewell dinner at the famous Windows On The World atop the World Trade Centre.

And now here he was, touching down in the UK for the first time in his life and heading to meet up with an old Aussie friend who now lived in Manchester.

"I was in Manchester for four days, and let's just say they were four very bizarre days," John says, with a slight shudder.

John's friend was living in a beautiful old house called Ladybarn Cottage. It was picture perfect, like something from a storybook.

"I arrived there on the evening of September 8, 2011," John recalls. "It was a lovely old cottage and my bedroom was at the very top of the stairs.

"I was so tired from travel, I thought I'd fall asleep instantly. But the moment I put my head down, my friend kept getting up and walking up and down the stairs.

"I remember thinking, 'Oh, she must be having a bit of a bad night. I hope she's okay,' then finally drifting off to sleep."

The following day, John and his friend enjoyed a happy time sightseeing throughout Manchester. John didn't think to ask his friend why she'd had such an unsettled night.

"After a beautiful dinner we returned to Ladybarn Cottage and pretty soon it was time for bed. Once the lights were out, the footsteps on the stairs started up again. Slow, determined footsteps, up the stairs to my door then down again.

"'Right,' I thought. 'I'm going to have to check on this.' The footsteps had been unrelenting. I opened the door to say, 'Hi, is everything okay?' but nobody was there. My friend's bedroom door was closed and there was nobody on the stairs. But the moment I closed the door, the footsteps started on the stairs again."

John says he didn't discuss the phantom footsteps with his old friend as he remembered her being easily spooked when they hung out together in Sydney.

"I didn't want to frighten her, and honestly I wasn't too worried. We enjoyed a great few days heading out to see the sights of Manchester, but each night the footsteps would return.

"On my second last day, I decided to stay in and have an easy day watching tele and relaxing on the couch. I kept seeing three lights in the shape of a triangle making their way across the living room wall. I dismissed these as being reflections from the car lights on the window. The cottage was close to the road. I just found the triangle light pattern interesting. People ask me was I spooked staying there, with the phantom footsteps and the mysterious lights. I say no. Did it freak me? No not at all. I actually found it more fascinating than scary. I just knew it was an old cottage so of course there would be something going on there. Ghosts and the paranormal don't scare me."

But John's final night atop the stairs at Ladybarn Cottage were fitful and disturbed to say the least.

"It was the 10th of September, I was going to London the next day. I was due in London to do a travel story on the Hempel Hotel.

"I went to bed and again… up and down, up and down came the footsteps. This time they kept me awake. They rattled me. I felt unsettled and I couldn't get to sleep. I must have finally drifted off at around 4am.

"I woke with a start at 11am as I had to be at the station at midday. I ran around the house hurriedly packing."

But something wasn't going to let John go without grabbing his attention one last time.

"The taxi had just beeped outside and I was making my way down the stairs for the last time," John recalls. "As I made my way to the door I could feel someone or something was trying to grab my attention, but I was in a hurry.

"I got in the taxi and the friendly driver said to me, 'Now, have you got everything.' For some reason, I replied, 'No, no I haven't.' And with that I went back, unlocked the door and went back into the house. I had my camera with me and I said, 'Whoever you are, I know you're here and it's okay and I acknowledge that you're here.' I picked up my camera and took a photograph of the bottom of the stairs because I knew something was there.

"Yes, I went back to the house, for that final goodbye to the ghost I didn't see."

Little did John realize that by the time he got off that train from Manchester to London and made his way to the hotel, the world would have changed and never be the same again. And for some strange reason, while travelling back from Manchester, John suddenly and inexplicably became overwhelmed with nausea.

"It just came on me. I hadn't eaten anything really except a piece of toast. It was the strangest most overwhelming feeling.

"I arrived at the hotel and everyone was on their phones," John recalls. "The Bellboy came and asked me how I was and I regaled him with my fun Manchester trip, but he looked somber.

"When I asked him how his day was, he quickly said, 'I'm really upset about what's happening in America.'

"I jokingly responded, 'Oh God, the Americans! What have they done this time?' He just looked at me, and said, 'You really don't know what's happened, do you? I can't begin to tell you. It's probably best I show you."

The Bellboy led John to his room. He turned on the television and News Footage showed the first tower of the World Trade Centre collapsing.

"I said to the Bellboy, 'Turn off the movie and tell me what's happening.' But the Bellboy looked at me soberly and said, 'Sir, that's not a movie, that is what's happening."

"I couldn't believe it. Only a week earlier I'd been feeling on top of the world at the top of that tower. It was too much to take in. Shortly after, I got the sad news that a friend of mine was in one of the hijacked planes. The one that crashed at the Pentagon."

John tried to put the horrors of September 11 behind him and continued on with his travels. He finished his trip off in Europe, came back through Asia and by October he was home.

He made a beeline for his local camera shop to put his holiday photos in for processing.

"We were still mostly using film then," he laughs. "When I went back to collect them, the lady said she needed to speak to me.

"John, we have a problem with one of your photos,' she said. 'We thought we had smudged it, but we hadn't. I think you better take a look.'

"She pulled out the photo and it was the last shot I took. The photo I went back into the house for. And there in the photo peeking around from behind the stairs was a little boy. And on the wall, those three lights that formed a triangle.

"I knew straight away the little boy was the presence I had addressed the morning I left, and he was the one walking up and down the steps.

"The day I was leaving, he really was trying to get my attention, but what was he trying to tell me?"

John racks his brain and tries to fathom the ghost child, the mysterious footsteps on the stairs, the strange lights, the events of September 11 and the fact that only a week early he'd been having the time of his life in the doomed World Trade Centre.

"I wish I could tell you what it all means," he says, shaking his head. "What was that little boy trying to tell me on the morning of September 11? Who is he and why the constant walking up and down the stairs? And what were those lights about?

"All I know is that I encountered a ghost during my stay in Manchester. It definitely was a haunted place. I just wish I knew what it all meant."

Adding to the mystery. When John went to get his photos of the mysterious boy beneath the stairs, all of his Manchester photos were missing.

"I honestly have no explanation," says John. "It is very unsettling. I think the missing photos have spooked me more than my one-on-one encounter with the actual ghost.

"It's surprising the photos went missing, but to me it felt like some sort of closure on a very disturbing and tragic time."

OTHER POPULAR HAUNTS IN MANCHESTER

Albert Hall: The popular venue is also the home of a poltergeist.

The Royal Exchange Theatre: Several sightings of actor and the theatre's founding artistic director James Maxwell. There is also a kind, motherly lady dressed in fine Victorian clothes often seen lurking in the foyer at interval.

Manchester Cathedral: In the late 1840s a young man was shocked to find his sister Fanny standing in the nave of the building. His sister lived many miles away in another village. When he called out to her, the woman suddenly vanished. The next day, the young man received news his sister Fanny had died. It was the exact time he'd seen her in the nave of the Cathedral.

Coronation Street set, Salford Quays. Filmed in and around Manchester. The cast and crew of the iconic soap, *Coronation Street*, insist the studio and set where it's filmed is haunted. The studio located next to Manchester Ship Canal is said to be inhabited by the ghosts of long-dead dock workers.

* * *

PRIN

PRINCESS' THEAT

MELBOURNE'S PRINCESS THEATRE, AUSTRALIA

You can feel his presence the moment you walk into Melbourne's beautiful Princess Theatre. The chill in the air denotes he is there.

Every day, every glittering night, as constant as the ghost light ever burning on the theatre's stage, he is there – waiting to take yet another standing ovation.

They say all theatres have ghosts. This 1854 Australian landmark boasts baritone Frederick Federici, he is Melbourne's very own phantom of the opera.

The sightings and encounters with Frederick are too many for his presence to be denied.

Acclaimed Melbourne photographer, Gina Milicia, was on assignment for a national magazine when she had a first-hand encounter with the ghost of Frederick.

"Myself and a journalist had been sent there specifically to talk about the ghost and photograph the beautiful theatre," Gina recalls. "And being the spiritual kind of person that I am, I was on edge before I even got there.

"When I walked in, I instantly felt the vibe was not great. An empty theatre always has a different energy about it anyway.

"I was asked to get an evocative shot of the beautiful stalls area. I started to set up; this was at a time when photographers were still using film. Do you know, I couldn't get my camera to work! Everything locked up in it. It was a manual camera – they don't lock up. But I couldn't get the film to roll on, I couldn't get it to advance. It just wouldn't work!"

Finally, the inexplicable glitch suddenly righted itself and Gina and the journalist were able to get on with covering the theatre ghost.

"Our guide was telling us that Frederick likes to sit in a particular seat," Gina explains. "The moment he said that, we heard a sudden thud and the seat in mention came snapping down. We all saw it! All the rest of the seats in the theatre were up and stayed up except for this particular seat."

Gina and the journalist shuddered at first and stared with wide-eyed disbelief at the seat. Nervously, they laughed it off as an elaborate joke being played on them.

"It was like, 'Ha, Ha! Very funny, now can we get back to business?' Gina says. "We went and checked under the seat looking for a pull wire, or we thought the seat may have been activated by remote control – but it wasn't.

"This ghost, this Frederick, was really showing himself to us and he was being playful."

The ghost's real name was Frederick Baker, but he went under the stage name of Frederick Federici. He was a gifted baritone and arrived in Australia from England in the mid-1880s to perform various operas.

He was in Melbourne for a production of Gounod's opera, Faust, at the Princess Theatre. The much-anticipated opening night was March 3, 1888 and Federici was playing the role of Mephistopheles.

This production of Faust ended dramatically with Mephistopheles sinking through a trapdoor into the fires of hell with his prize, the tragic Faust.

This finale on opening night proved more dramatic than anticipated. On his descent, the audience noticed that Federici was slumped over slightly. Unbeknownst to the audience and cast, he had suffered a heart attack and died on his descent into "hell".

The unknowing cast happily returned to the stage for the curtain call and to take their triumphant bows. It wasn't until after they had all left the stage and the curtain came down they were told that Fred was dead! The spooky thing was that everyone at the performance said they saw Frederick taking his bows. The cast insisted he was on the stage with them for the ovation. And since that tumultuous opening night, Fred's ghost has never left the theatre.

"That story never ceases to give me goose bumps," Gina says. "I honestly could not wait to get out of there, it just felt so uncomfortable. I wasn't scared as such as I have encountered so many ghosts in my life. But knowing the story, I just felt so shocked by what we'd experienced.

"I don't know why I reacted like that – as I say, I have had many ghostly encounters. Our guide also insisted he is a friendly ghost and she also candidly told us how many well-known actors have had their own close encounter with Frederick while appearing in some of the big productions throughout the years."

Bert Newton, Marina Prior, Lisa McCune are just some of the stars who have rubbed shoulders with Fred. And many of the staff at the theatre have had their experiences.

"Our guide said they all acknowledge him, and he's very friendly and just wants to be around the action," Gina laughs.

He has been reported as a "benevolent presence" and as a "friendly poltergeist."

"That's all well and good," says Gina, good-naturedly. "All I know is we couldn't wait to get out of that theatre. It felt really uncomfortable, it WAS really scary. I had already worked myself into a lather before going there. But when that seat dropped – Frederick's seat – I totally freaked.

"Let's just say, as we made our way back to our car there was a lot of 'Holy shit! What the hell? and Oh my God's!' pouring from our mouths!

* * *

POWIS CASTLE, UNITED KINGDOM

Grave and foreboding against the grey skies of Wales, this imposing castle beckons to those looking for a haunting.

Dating back to 1200, Powis Castle was once a military headquarters before it took up its major role as a grand home for wealthy families.

There are countless reports of ghosts and supernatural happenings occurring within the castle's walls and its impressive, sprawling surrounds.

Chief among the supernatural sightings is the story of the gentleman ghost who came calling three times in one day.

An elderly lady – a highly-respected seamstress – had been asked to come to the castle to carry out some of her specialized work.

Her work would keep her at the castle for a few days so she was given a small bedroom where she could base herself and be comfortable. What the then owners of Powis Castle didn't tell her was the bedroom, despite its cheery and clean appearance, was mysteriously haunted.

The first night passed event free. But the next evening, as she sat reading her Bible, a gentleman came to her door. He walked in and strolled to the window to admire the view. Without a word, or a tipping of his hat to acknowledge the startled seamstress, he strode out of the bedroom.

Somewhat shaken and perturbed by the visit, it occurred to the lady she had just in fact seen a ghost. The way he appeared without a noise, the way he seemed lost in his own world and hadn't even flinched at seeing the startled woman staring gobsmacked at his surprise visit and his sudden departure. The way he had made not one single sound left her convinced her room was haunted.

Shivering with fright, she quickly grabbed her Bible, and clutching it tight, began to pray.

No sooner had she focused her thoughts on heavenly places, the door opened again and in strode the gentleman caller. This time he came and stood behind her, almost as if he were posing with the woman for a photograph. She could see it all being played out in a mirror.

The woman spun around to look at the phantom guest but he quickly exited the room.

That night after much praying and fitful walking the floor, the woman mustered the courage to prepare for bed. Just as she was about to change into her nightgown, the ghostly gentleman reappeared. The nerve-worn woman mustered the courage to ask him what was it that he wanted.

This time the ghost acknowledged the woman. He beckoned for her to follow him, and nervously she did. He led her to another small room, similar to the one she had been attempting to sleep in. The ghost directed the woman to lift up a floorboard and remove a tin box. Then the ghost took her to a crevice in the wall where the key to the box was hidden.

The woman, still barely believing she was standing in the presence of a ghost, was told she was to dispatch the box to the Earl of Powis in London. The ghost assured the woman that if she carried out his instructions, he would never appear again.

The quiet seamstress not only completed her work at the castle the next day, she also managed to fulfill the ghost's request and have the box shipped to the Earl of Powis.

The Earl was said to be overjoyed upon receiving the box. He immediately gave strict instructions the unassuming seamstress was to be handsomely looked after for the rest of her days.

No one knows what exactly was in the box, many say it was the legal deeds to the castle which enabled the Earl to take up his rightful place.

And as for the gentleman ghost, his identity is forever a mystery. Why did he choose the seamstress to reveal the mysterious box that changed the course of the life of the Earl of Powis and indeed her humble life forever? No one will ever know. One thing is certain, true to his word, he has not been sighted at the castle ever since.

His presence has been felt and is regarded as benign. Other

specters, not as friendly, have set up home in the many rooms of the looming castle.

The Duke's Room and the Ballroom Wing are reported to see the most ghostly activity. A refined lady dressed stylishly in black has been seen sitting in a chair by the fireplace in the Duke's Room. One visitor said they felt a woman's hand running her fingers playfully up and down their arm.

The piano in the Ballroom has been heard playing in the dead of night and a piano stool has been seen to move seemingly by itself.

Frightened guests have consistently reported knocks on their bedroom door and windows and, when tended to, find there is nobody there.

And out in the sprawling grounds, a child dressed in a green velvet suit has been seen disappearing up a tree.

As for the seamstress, people believe because she had such a happy and fulfilled life after following the instructions of the Gentleman ghost, she died peacefully and crossed over into the next life without the need to remain as a tormented ghost.

The romantic like to believe the Gentleman ghost was waiting for her on the other side and their spirits travel happily through eternity together.

LLANCAIACH FAWR, CAERPHILLY, WALES.
A HOUSE TEEMING WITH GHOSTS

This grand old home, built over a medieval dwelling in 1550, has enjoyed the freaky moniker of being one of the most haunted places in the United Kingdom.

Pretty as a picture, Llancaiach Fawr at first glance doesn't look like the dwelling for a multitude of ghosts – but it is.

As the evening shadows come crawling, the home takes on a somber and sinister appearance.

Around this time, visitors have reported seeing the petticoat-wearing housekeeper Mattie, who is said to have died tragically in one of the bedrooms. Others have seen a troubled little boy who crankily tugs at the hair and sleeves of spooked visitors.

Each floor has been given the going-over by countless paranormal investigators and their astonishing photos have revealed a multitude of orbs and shadow figures. Such is the overwhelming activity, locals call the handsome house the House of Ghosts.

The ghostly lodgers are said to be presided over by the spirit of the original Llancaiach Fawr owner, Edward Pritchard, who is often seen at dusk strolling the grounds neatly attired in his Civil War outfit.

THE GHOST OF RED MARY, LEAMANEH CASTLE, IRELAND

The ruins of Leamaneh Castle are imposing and compelling to the eye. It simply screams 'haunted'. And indeed it is.

Emerging from the ancient crumblings, an apparition of a bedraggled red-haired woman has been seen. The woman strides about the ruins of the 1648-built manor house, her screams and scornful cackles echoing off the limestone.

This is the ghost of Mary McMahon, also known as Maire Rua, which literally means Red Mary. Mary's hair, as red as dripping blood, suited her brazen femme fatale nature.

From the moment her first husband Daniel O'Neillan died, leaving her an immense fortune, Mary lived an ostentatious life of self-indulgent plenty.

It was her inherited wealth that allowed her to build the manor house which was dubbed one of Ireland's finest Tudor mansions in the 17th century. The four-story-high gabled mansion house was artfully added on to the original 1480-built limestone tower.

Mary lived in the mansion house, ruling the roost with her second husband Connor O'Brien.

From all accounts, this red-haired harridan was a force to be reckoned with. In 1651, Cromwell's armies invaded Ireland and plundered the place. Mary's husband Connor bravely put up a fight but was severely wounded.

A small band of loyal soldiers carried Connor back to the castle, thinking he might benefit from the tenderness and loving care of his wife.

But the moment she lay eyes on her ailing husband, Mary was anything but loving or tender.

"What use have I for a dead man?" she is said to have screamed from the tower. Incensed by the sight of critically-injured Connor, Mary hastened his death by throwing him from the tower.

Far from being grief stricken or tormented by guilt for her murderous action, Mary bathed, got dressed up to the nines and went off to Limerick to flirt and ensnare her third husband, John Cooper. Ironically, Cooper was a Cromwellian officer, the mob who killed Connor.

Crazy, fiery Red Mary soon got fed up with Cooper and she is said to have cunningly and quickly dispatched him by pushing him out of a third-story window.

Mary was convinced each of her husbands were purely after her vast wealth. By the time she died, she was said to have had 25 husbands who she killed off in all manner of imaginative and sadistic ways. She forced one poor spouse to ride his horse over the nearby cliffs of Moher. Well, she actually had him tied to the horse, and she deliberately frightened the horse and personally chased the terrified creature over the cliffs.

But Red Mary didn't reserve her boundless cruelty to her seemingly endless stream of husbands. She kept a harem of male servants. If any male servants displeased her they were hung from the castle tower, which seemed to give Mary a surge of pleasure.

She would often stand before her ill-fated servant and taunt him with her high-pitched and annoying cackle. She is said to have loved the terror in their eyes as she prolonged the inevitable – a painful and slow death.

If the man-servants thought they had it bad, Mary saved her most appalling sadism for her terrified female servants. Any servant sent to work for Mary usually knew they wouldn't be leaving Leamaneh Castle alive.

Any female servant found displeasing to Mary for any number of trivial misdemeanors would be brought before their enraged mistress. Mary, her electric red hair all but standing on end, would seize a sword from its scabbard, tear the blouses off her screaming-for-mercy and petrified servants and cut off their breasts.

Writhing in agony and bleeding to death, Mary would laugh uproariously as the doomed female servants suffered one last and prolonged painful indignity – being hung by their hair. Mary would drink and cavort at the foot of her hanging servants. Relishing their agony, taunting them over how they were soon to die.

But karma would catch up with the sadistic and psychotic Mary. Her bizarre and cruel actions had earned her many enemies. A group of enraged neighbors seized Mary and sealed her alive in a hollow tree trunk. Her screams and pleas for mercy were heard for weeks. Slowly as she starved to death, the screams faded until no sound could be heard from the hollow tree.

Her gruesome death condemned her to forever haunt the ruins of the grisly Leamaneh Castle – a place she had treated as a gluttonous playground of sadistic torture and murder. It is said the ghosts of the many she murdered chase her terrified spirit throughout the ruins, surrounding her then inflicting on her the many barbaric acts she subjected them to.

The ghost of Red Mary is said to be the most tormented spirit in all of Ireland. And that her torture will be eternal.

By the time she died entombed in the hollow tree, Mary was said to have had at least 12 children. Her son Donagh O'Brien, was the last of her clan to occupy the haunted castle. He was known as the richest commoner in Ireland. He is said to have attempted to flee the ceaseless hauntings of his mother by moving to the larger Dromoland Castle in Newmarket-on-Fergus.

DUCKETT'S GROVE CASTLE, COUNTY CARLOW IRELAND
Everyone is familiar with the saying "scream like a banshee". Well, Duckett Grove Castle has its very own, and boy can she let rip with a blood-curdling scream.

For those not in the know, a banshee is a figure from Irish and Scottish folklore. It is an ancestral ghost and warns family members of approaching death with a guttural wail or scream.

In the case of the Duckett family, the ghostly banshee is believed to be a woman with whom William Duckett was carrying on an affair. She died while riding her horse on the Duckett grounds. Following her death, her incensed mother put a curse on the Duckett family and the legend of the Duckett banshee was born.

The banshee and her screams have been reported all over the extensive Duckett property. There was one particularly horrific period where her wails went on for two days straight. No one dared approach, but eyewitnesses said the incessant wailing came from the ruined towers of the castle.

A number of those unfortunate enough to hear the banshee have within days gone on to experience a death as is the tradition of the banshee.

Along with the dreaded banshee, many ghosts from the Duckett family also haunt the castle ruins. Many believe because of the curse put on them by the banshee's mother, the Duckett family members can never be at peace in death. And with the ghosts have also come reports of phantom voices, apparitions and mysterious lights.

The castle has also featured on the popular American paranormal show, *Destination Truth*, which explored the castle ruins and confirmed many of the paranormal sightings.

The ruins are now often the backdrop for many popular community events including fairs and flower shows.

But to get the full haunted effect, the castle is best experienced on sombre grey days where you can wander the grounds virtually alone. Just you and the wind and a few phantom members of the Duckett family.

It truly is a haunted place, but beware the cry of the banshee, for if you hear her cry you may... well, we all know what happens to people who listen to banshees. Freak out!

* * *

SEXTANTIO – MEDIEVAL VILLAGE, ITALY

"It is nothing short of breathtaking. Hard to imagine it actually exists. It's picture postcard perfect. Like something out of a Fairytale book."

Such is the usual enthusiastic gushing associated with seeing a picture of the historical village of Santo Stefano di Sessanio, or Sextantio as it is called these days.

If a simple picture can have that effect on people, wait until you experience this fortified medieval village in person.

Acclaimed photographer Gina Milicia and her friend Carmel Ruggeri couldn't believe their eyes when they first saw pictures of Sextantio.

Carmel had just led another successful jaunt through Sicily for her business, Sicilian Food Tours. Gina had joined the tour to conduct photographic workshops – and now the two mates were in need of some serious R and R.

"It had been a good tour, but hectic and we were exhausted," Gina explains. "We were making our way back to Rome when we decided to give ourselves a reward by staying a night at Sextantio.

"Carmel's friends had all raved about the place and as soon as I saw the pictures, I knew we had to go there. It just looked amazing – a photographer's dream.

"For me, the place was all the more special because it looked just like the village my family hail from in Sicily. It had a real home vibe; I couldn't wait to go."

Located in the mountains of Abruzzo at 1,250 meters above sea level, inside the Gran Sasso and Monti della Laga national park, the village with its grandiose perimeter wall is a classic example of an Italian medieval hill town. It has been largely restored and is now a thriving weekend and summer retreat. It is favored by visitors from Rome which is just 150 kilometers to the north.

Incredibly, the town fell upon hard times and the peasant population left the walled city en masse. Bizarrely, this once-buzzing locale became a ghost town. But the abandonment did serve a good purpose – left alone, the town was saved from architectural abuse – it kept its original Medieval charm without being bastardized by blow-ins.

"The whole village is pretty well as it was, but they've turned it into a five- or six-star resort," Gina explains. "You're staying in peasant houses as they were, they've just spruced things up – re-done the bathrooms; there's lovely white-washed walls. It's just immaculate.

"When we drove in, I gasped and said, 'Oh, I can't believe this. This place is amazing!'"

But Carmel fell silent and her stony expression clearly showed she wasn't feeling the same way as Gina.

"I'm completely creeped out," Carmel said as an excited Gina opened a tiny medieval window and was knocked out by the view.

"'What's wrong with you?' I said with disbelief. 'This place is beautiful, I feel like I'm at my Nona's house. It's amazing. Come on, come here and look at this incredible view.'"

Gina got lost in her own enthusiasm while Carmel shivered and felt completely uneasy.

"I was trying to talk her around, pointing out all the fantastic rustic features. I mean here we were in a medieval peasant's house, the furniture is all authentic, the original beds are all stuffed with straw. It's authentic but it's all five star.

"And all the while Carmel is shaking her head and repeating her mantra about being 'creeped out'. In the end she looked at me and shrugged and said, 'I'm going to the pub. I need a drink.'"

No sooner had Carmel gone, Gina set to catching up on some work.

"I thought it would be nice to have some quiet time and catch up on a few things," Gina recalls. "But then suddenly I started getting completely freaked out too. I remember thinking to myself, 'What's wrong?' I just didn't feel right. I looked around the room and I felt terrible.

"I remember thinking, 'I'm not here on my own anymore.' All the hairs on the back of my neck stood up and they stayed up.

"You know when there's someone watching you and you feel

totally creeped out? That's how it felt. I honestly have never felt like that before, never felt so scared. I'm very sensitive to spirits and they don't usually scare me. I've had so many encounters with ghosts, but this was an overwhelming sense of evil."

Gina tried to lighten her mood by telling herself she was overreacting.

"I was there trying to talk myself out of this black feeling," she says. "I remember saying, 'You're all nervy because of the ideas Carmel's sewed into your head.' Try as I might, I just could not shift the sense of foreboding. I couldn't settle myself down."

Gina even baulked at going upstairs to her bedroom to get something from her bag.

"I can't remember what it was, but it took me about twenty minutes to summon the courage to walk up the stairs because I was so incredibly creeped out," she says.

"I finally bolted up the stairs, got whatever it was that I needed from my bag, then I just ran. I literally fled the house."

Gina ran through the labyrinth of ancient cobblestone streets trying to find Carmel. Carmel was where she said she'd be: at the pub!

A breathless Gina sat down and tried to explain to her friend that she too was now "creeped out" but couldn't exactly explain why.

"See, I told you," Carmel said, pouring herself another drink. "I don't want to go back into that house."

Gina says the two of them spent much of the night making up stories and egging each other on.

"We were saying things like, 'I wonder how many people have been murdered in that house.' It was scary, but it was fun at the same time.

"The reality was we both felt that not many pleasant experiences were had in that house.

"Don't get me wrong – the resort was lovely, the staff were amazing, the whole resort was beautiful, but there was something sinister in that house.

"We didn't hear voices, we didn't see anything, but we just wanted to get out of there. It really is a photographer's paradise. I mean, you have access to a medieval village that isn't swarming with a million tourists, so you have all these beautiful empty laneways and alleyways, but I just wanted to leave.

"That sense of fear and dread was strongest in the house, but I felt it everywhere. The pub and the breakfast room were the only areas that had a good energy."

The two friends spoke through the night and couldn't wait for sunrise to come.

"Normally when you stay in a beautiful resort like that you go for a late checkout because you want to soak it up, lounge around and be there as long as possible," Gina laughs. "We checked out at 7am! I have never checked out of somewhere so early. We'd only arrived at 6pm the previous night. It's the fastest I have left anywhere. We were on the road by five past seven. We really had nowhere to be, just knew we didn't want to be there. We just couldn't deal with it."

* * *

THE EDINBURGH VAULTS, UNITED KINGDOM

It's little wonder the Edinburgh Vaults are considered the most haunted place in Scotland.

The Vaults are a series of chambers formed in the arches of the South Bridge which were completed in 1788. It was here in the sinister shadows that tradesmen and Scotland's criminal underbelly existed side by side for over 30 years.

Illicit material, including the bodies of people killed by notorious serial killers Burke and Hare for medical experiments, were also stored in The Vaults.

Adding to the dank atmosphere, huge cracks began to appear in the South Bridge, allowing every bit of putrid runoff from the overcrowded city to seep into the vault's lower levels – this made spending any length of time there, let alone living there, almost impossible.

But some had no choice. By 1845, Edinburgh was overflowing with Irish immigrants desperately escaping the potato famine. Slum lords weren't shy to take advantage of their hopelessness, and the vaults quickly became a place where families could find shelter. Sadly, there would often be up to 10 people "living" in dark, cramped spaces that really were only meant for one.

Before long, the vaults became the area's red light district, a maze of illicit pubs and brothels. There was no police presence, so debauchery, rape and murder were the rampant order of the day. And the ghosts of such low life can very much be felt at the Vaults today. There have been far too many close encounters for there to be any doubt. Visitors have reported everything from hearing taunting, threatening voices to seeing full-on, clear-as-day apparitions.

Emma Surgenor from Blackpool got the shock of her life when she looked back over her photos following a visit to the Vaults.

Emma had gone on a nighttime tour with her sister and taken copious amounts of photos.

"Some of the photos came up pitch black and others came through," Emma told the UK Mirror. "We went through all the photos on my digital camera that evening and lightened up the pictures that came back black.

"To our shock, this figure which looked like a man appeared in one of them. We got a chill sensation and just screamed 'Oh my God.' It was a creepy moment. My sister was petrified. She was going on about how he was standing right behind her. Then she thought it was pretty cool. It's pretty scary stuff. There was definitely no one else there when I took that photo."

The disturbing photo shows a man standing incredibly close behind Emma's sister. He is wearing what appears to be a long coat and boots. Emma believes the figure may be a ghost widely known as 'The Watcher' or 'Mr. Boots.'

"There are a lot of stories about a man down there who wears big boots and a coat," she said. "There's another called 'The Watcher' with long hair and 18th century clothing.

"To think my sister was standing there right next to him and she and I didn't even know it. It has completely creeped us out."

The Watcher or Mr. Boots has been seen by hundreds of terrified visitors to the Vaults. He has consistently been described as tall with no eyes, a full beard, a long coat and big thigh-high boots.

Some reports suggest he watches visitors from the corridor and can be protective of the wall in one of the smaller vaults, sometimes shouting "get out", when people go near it.

Another famous spirit that many visitors to the Vaults encounter is a young boy named Jack. The ghost of Jack is notorious for grabbing hold of visitors' hands as they explore the wine vault. Many say they have heard his scurrying footsteps following behind them as they furtively make their way along the darkened corridors.

But the scariest vault of all is known as the "occult chamber", known to be used for years by hundreds of dark souls dabbling in the occult. It is understood the room was regarded as a space for evil rituals. There are rumors that a woman was sacrificed there on a stone slab by members of a satanic sect after they had tortured her for days.

It's been reported that in 2003 a BBC Radio Producer, Debbie McPhail, accompanied the Edinburgh Vaults' owner into the tunnels to record an interview. The interview was not about the paranormal, but the ghosts had other ideas. When Debbie was playing the tape back she was shocked to hear a new voice, one that wasn't there at the interview, telling them to "get out".

"When I was listening back to it, I could hear Norrrie Rowan (the vault owner) chatting and then I heard another voice," Debbie told reporters. "It was close by to the microphone because you can tell if voices are far away or not. I knew it wasn't the presenter or Norrie because the voice had a slightly Irish accent. But I couldn't understand why no one responded to it.

"When the presenter came back up I asked him who they had met in the vault and he said nobody. My husband thought it could be Gaelic and I asked a colleague who spoke the language and she said they could be saying 'get out' or 'go away'. I have no reason to doubt it. You could sit forever and make explanations for it, but it's there on the disc and that's good enough for me."

Despite the promised terror a visit to the Vaults guarantees, tourists and lovers of the paranormal flock to the site in their droves, making it one of Edinburgh's most popular tourist attractions and earning it the name of Scotland's most haunted place.

* * *

THE GAP, AUSTRALIA

It's a place of brutal beauty. Veiled in sea spray, its gnarled cliffs are mercilessly and forever battered with a constant screaming soundtrack hurled up by a seemingly scorned Pacific Ocean.

The tourists who flock here almost run up the final trail of 25 sandstone steps, eager to get closer to the edge. White knuckled and clutching the safety rail, they stare into the vast expanse, turning their backs and barely noticing the perfect view of Sydney behind them.

Many have also come here to say 'goodbye cruel world' and turn their backs on life. Countless lives hurled to the sea and rocks below make the Gap a harbinger of tragedy and a truly haunted place.

Welcome to The Gap, Sydney's infamous "drop off" point, a sweeping arc of wave-blasted sandstone gouged into South Head. Long before the Sydney Harbour Bridge arched its steely back over the majestic harbor, way before the white tiles of the Opera house gleamed and shuddered above the soaring voice of Dame Joan Sutherland, this majestic sweep of coastline, more than 100 m high in places, played lively in the 'imaginations of locals.' It still does.

The Gap is a place of intense contrasts. Stand at the safety rail, look straight out to sea and the full brunt of nature hurtles towards you. The noise, a screaming fury, almost knocks you over. Turn around and the harbor and city skyline are displayed in all their glory. And, like the contrasting views, life and death manage to coexist here.

Ask a Sydneysider their impressions of the Gap and they'll tell you it's lunch in the sun at Doyles and a beer at the Watsons Bay Hotel. They'll say it's the best vantage point from which to catch the start of the Sydney to Hobart yacht race. And, either in hushed tones or with insensitive grins, they'll tell you, "It's where people go to jump."

Indeed, the great unspoken has been associated with the Gap since the mid-1800s. The first recorded case of someone taking their own life here was of 35-year-old Anne Harrison, a publican's wife who leapt to her death in 1863 after grieving for her nephew who fell from the cliff top.

But two plaques, nailed to the hard wood safety fence, detailing phone numbers for Lifeline and The Salvation Army, serve as a reminder of recent tragedies.

There was the man who, in 1993, murdered his former girlfriend then tried to end his own life by driving off the Gap at great speed. "He meant business," Stuart McKinlay, a carpenter, then working for the Woollahra Council and making regular repairs to the safety fence, told me.

"He tore down here at a million miles an hour, smashed through the fence and became airborne over Jacob's Ladder – that part of the Gap where the rock fishermen clamber down."

The car flipped mid-flight and became wedged on a ledge. Miraculously, the man survived. "He's in jail now. They called us straight away to fix the fence."

That fence – a sturdy hardwood affair mostly waist-high and wrapped in cyclone mesh – is intended to prevent people from getting too close to that dramatic beauty. But as Stuart and his mate and co-worker Bill McLeary told me, those wanting to be at one with the view will not be hindered by a barrier.

"People come up here for the view. As you can see, it's spectacular," Stuart said. "Sadly it's also a well-known place for the obvious reason," he says before falling silent. "Um… people like to jump. It still goes on but it's kept real quiet."

How appropriate that the master of the cliffhanger, Alfred Hitchcock should also find himself drawn to the ominous cliffs of the Gap.

It was a windy Friday, the 6th of May 1960, and Hitch was in Sydney for the Australian premiere of his ultimate classic, Psycho.

While the maestro film director didn't say he felt the Gap was haunted, he told the Sun Herald it was the perfect place to make one of his trademark thrillers.

"He took an umbrella with him," wrote journalist David Burke. "'Just in case I float over the edge,' he explained. 'Before I make a picture I must always experience the hero's emotion myself.'

"He poised his roly poly figure on a railing of the safety fence and looked down on the rocks hundreds of feet below. The westerly blew his umbrella inside out; the renowned chins and jowl quivered with the cold but his eyes lit up to saucer-like proportions.

"'Yes, a really ideal setting for suspense.'"

The Gap again became a focal point for horror and suspense with the discovery of the body of model Caroline Bryne's body awash in white foam and wedged between rocks at the cliff base on June 8, 1995.

Caroline worked as a modeling instructor for legendary Sydney deportment and etiquette educator June Dally-Watkins.

At first, police assumed Caroline was just another Gap suicide statistic, but thanks to some keen sleuthing by June Dally-Watkins, Gordon Wood – Caroline's then boyfriend and chauffeur to high profile businessman, Rene Rivkin – was charged with her murder. He was found guilty in an explosive murder trial on 21 November 2008 and spent three years in Goulburn jail. He was later acquitted of the conviction in February 2012.

Caroline's spirit is said to be one of many troubled souls whose desperate screams can be heard calling in the dead of night along the wind-blasted cliffs of the Gap.

Bill Fahey remembered being called out to the Gap a couple of times a week when he was with the Police Department's Cliff Rescue Squad from 1955 to 1985.

"It was mostly suicides," he said. "I always told anyone who was feeling down in the dumps to hold on because a new day will bring change; hold on and wait for the new day."

Bill singled out one particularly macabre incident in the early '60s that haunted him through the years. "A bloke had pushed his three children off then thrown himself over," he said. "There were four bodies at the base of the cliff and we had to go and bring them back up. We got down there and there was this fisherman who just casually stepped over the bodies and kept right on with his fishing. I've never seen such single-minded behavior in my life."

Gap historian Claire McIntyre felt so close to those who'd taken their lives there she wrote a book about them. "They're not just obscure people who've jumped, they're people like us," she said.

The former director of nursing believes the Gap is a very haunted place. "Just to be there is a spiritual experience," she said. "There's a definite draw; you can't ignore it. As I got more involved in the writing of the book, my daughter was concerned that I was disturbing the dead. I totally disagreed. As far as I'm concerned, these people have a story and they are not just a statistic. I think I'm helping to put them to sleep."

Residents of the area moved here to enjoy the ceaseless roar of the ocean and that view. They didn't intend to be caught up in the broken lives of others or to become heroes. But that is what has happened to some over the years. In the 1960s, Mrs. Eve Bettke and her husband Anthony were known as "The Guardians Of the Gap". Together they brought scores of people back from the edge. In one week alone they dragged back 27 people. News reports from the time tell how the Bettkes, who once lived across the road, kept a vigil from their house, scouring the cliffs for anyone lurking too near the edge. Often they'd invite potential suicides back to their house for a comforting chat.

Don Ritchie lived in Watson's Bay all his life until his passing in 2012 at the age of 85. In that time he saved 160 people from jumping to their deaths at the Gap. Some of the people he saved sent him thank-you cards and went on to enjoy normal, happy lives. Like the Bettkes before him, Don kept a steady watch over the Gap from his house and climbed over the fence to sit and comfort the troubled who were only centimeters away from ending their lives.

When I spoke to Don back in 2000, he preferred to dwell on the Gap's positive stories.

"There's often people playing musical instruments in the park," he said. "And the music wafts up over the cliffs. It sounds beautiful against the sounds of the ocean."

But the music is often heard tinkling up and down the cliffs long after the musicians have downed instruments and left the park.

Many claim to hear bagpipes, others drums. Some say they hear singing.

But more than music, many visitors say they have seen people with horror-stricken faces looking up through the mist of the waves on the rocks below. Others all say the moment they look over the Gap they hear terrified screaming.

It is believed the screams belong to the tormented victims of the ill-fated ship, the Dunbar. The Dunbar was wrecked in pounding seas on the rocks at the foot of the Gap after travelling for 81 days from England. Of the 122 aboard, only one survived – 15-year-old able seaman James Johnson.

The ghosts of the Dunbar are believed to linger at the foot of Gap, forever screaming over the waves. Others have seen an old seaman weeping at the Dunbar's anchor which is incorporated into a memorial at the top of the cliff.

People do mind the Gap. They fear it, because they know it to be a disturbing – yet beautiful – haunted place.

* * *

THE GHOST PIERS OF BRIGHTON, UNITED KINGDOM

She hovers darkly on her silhouetted stilts, a mere shadow of the grand dame she used to be.

Forlorn, fragile and shaken, she appears as one who tore her lace ball gown after too good a night out. And let's face it, she saw many a good night out.

As Joan Crawford once famously said of Marilyn Monroe, "She was the good time had by all." The same can be said of Brighton's West Pier Ballroom.

The dance began in 1866 and it seems the band played on through various wars, the comings and goings of five monarchs – books were written about her, fashion and music trends came and went – until the tragic, tattered and tired last waltz in 1975.

By then, Brighton's West Pier and her once-glittering ballroom was showing its age; she had fallen into dereliction and disrepair.

Those who loved the Victorian structure fought to save her, but a pounding storm in 2002 all but knocked the grand dame off her feet. The walkway leading to the concert hall partially collapsed. Soon after, another storm came calling and smashed the concert hall into the sea.

Two fires, one believed to be deliberately lit, sealed her fate in 2003, but the remnants of the Grand Ballroom refused to give in. Gaunt and broken, she hasn't quite surrendered to the unrelenting ravages of the sea.

Most Brighton locals look to the skeletal remains of the Ballroom and each has a nostalgic memory. They were told sea air was a tonic, so they would promenade the vast boardwalk drinking in deep drafts of salty goodness. Others recall the many sideshows, the kiosks selling Brighton Rock, the green- and white-striped deckchairs. There were the lavish balls, the music being played by the pier's resident orchestra.

Many locals swear that if you stand on nearby Brighton Palace Pier and look to the wonderfully gloomy remains of the West Pier Ballroom you can hear the faint restrains of the old orchestra still playing, the haunting notes being carried across the dark waters on the wind.

Others swear they have seen spectral couples lost in an eternal dance out there on the crumbling timbers of the once lavish Victorian Pleasure Palace.

"Of course the place is haunted," chastises one passionate local. "You just think of how many thousands flocked to the piers of Brighton with its cafés, ballrooms and funfairs in its heyday.

"All those people would be dead now and many of their spirits for some reason would be trapped out there in the old ballroom or even along the Palace Pier. Not only on the old piers but all through Brighton. After all, they say Brighton is the most haunted city in all of England."

And he's not joking. All through Brighton and its surrounds, the locals abound with tales of harrowing hauntings and unexplained ghostly encounters. Forget the fun of the Ghost Train out on the pier – you only have to wander the streets to be told stories that bring out the goose bumps and make your hair stand on end.

Ghosty investigators, ParanormalDatabase.com, maintain there have been at least 129 reported incidents of spooky activity in and around the winding streets of Brighton in the last few years alone. More chilling, many eyewitnesses have reported seeing the same apparitions and in the same place, time and again.

Among the chilling stories:

The Pale Woman Vanishes: Parishioners at All Saints Church, Patcham, Brighton, recall a wan woman, grey of complexion, appearing in one of the pews during a Christmas service. A kind gentleman took pity on the sickly lady and placed his coat around her shoulders, hoping to keep her warm. The moment he placed the coat upon her gaunt shoulders, the lady vanished.

Three Phantom Nuns: The manager of a shop in North Street

Brighton reported seeing three phantom nuns come calling. He met them with a smile, but they didn't seem to see him. They reportedly glided across the shop floor before vanishing through the back wall.

The Sad Child In Pajamas: Folk around the Library in Brighton have reported seeing a ghostly child dressed in pajamas and carrying a wooden toy. It is believed the child was killed during a World War II bombing raid. No one has reported seeing the child since the last of the bomb-damaged buildings were fully demolished in the 1990s.

The Lady In The White Dress and The Soldier In Red: Actors at the Brighton Dome Theatre on the New Road have little doubt their performance space is haunted. While rehearsing for various productions, they have been visited by a spectral woman with a lavish bouffant hairstyle and wearing a long white dress. As if that wasn't frightening enough, they have noticed a soldier in a red tunic passing behind the curtains. Along with these two ghostly visitors, the actors have been spooked by that ultimate classic of haunting sounds: phantom footsteps and rattling chains.

The Lurking Coach Driver: Patrons at the Brighton Rocks Pub have seen a man in a cloak drifting around the front door of this popular watering hole. The cloaked figure has also been seen hovering through the gentlemen's toilets. It is understood this phantom was the driver of the local mayor and he was murdered shortly after leaving the pub. Chillingly, cupboards within the hotel held shut by bricks have flung themselves open and heavy filing cabinets have inexplicably fallen over. The pub's dog has often become terrified for no reason, or on other occasions, begins playing happily with something unseen.

Screams From The Tunnel: The Clayton tunnel was the scene of a horrific train crash on August 25, 1861. The tragedy occurred as a result of a miscommunication between two signalmen. Their mistake caused two trains to enter the tunnel on the same track. 23 people, amid screams and the crunching of metal, were killed that day. The tunnel is without doubt a very haunted place. Even today, locals maintain they can hear the agonized screams of passengers who died in the tragedy along with the high-pitch screeching of crunching metal echoing frightfully from the tunnel. The cottage located above the tunnel entrance and where the signalman John

Brown was posted at the time of the accident is also haunted. "Troubled voices," have been heard coming from the cottage.

The writer Charles Dickens was also clearly haunted by the train collision in the Clayton Tunnel. His 1866 short story *The Signal Man* tells of a ghostly apparition that appears to a signalman near a tunnel. The ghost makes regular visits to the signal man, who realizes he is being warned of an impending disaster that will occur in the tunnel. Many believe the ghost of Dickens himself haunts the lonely cottage above the Clayton Tunnel.

* * *

THE HAUNTED SKYSCRAPER, THAILAND

Foreboding and forbidden, this shadowy 49-story skyscraper is known by locals as Bangkok's Tower of Terror.

Many say the building is cursed. It looms large yet broken and decaying while offering majestic views of the vibrant city and the breathtaking Chao Phraya River.

Due to a number of horrific deaths within the building, ghost watchers, the ghoulish and the downright curious flock to the tower to wander the shadowy floors in the hope they will encounter a ghost.

"You hear of haunted houses, but not entire skyscrapers," says keen ghost watcher, Neil Treloar, who has been "trespassing" in the freaky tower for over two years now. The English-born accountant defies the authorities by "breaking into the building" and conducting impromptu ghost tours.

"We risk being arrested, but our desire for ghost hunting keeps us coming back to the tower," Neil, 37, says. "It's not for the faint hearted. It takes it out of you climbing all 49 stories; you don't know who or what is going to be lurking around the next corner. And all the while we're looking back over our shoulder in case the police are coming to arrest us for trespassing.

"News of the ghost tours is spread via social media and word of mouth. Lately, the owners of the building have stepped up security, so it's getting harder and harder to get inside the Tower of Terror."

Officially known as the Sathorn Unique Building, it was going to be Bangkok's premium tower of luxury. The ultimate in high-end apartment living.

Asia's wealthiest, along with a smattering of Middle Eastern oil barrens, were clamoring to secure themselves a swanky pad in the 49-story gilded skyscraper.

Proving that all that glitters is certainly not gold, this massive construction project was suddenly abandoned due to the collapse of the Thai Baht during the nightmare that was the 1997 Asian Financial Crisis.

Totally abandoned, the unfinished skyscraper soon began to rot with the telltale signs of dereliction. Rather than being a beacon of luxury for the elite, its residents are now a sinister mixed bunch of homeless, drug addicts, vagrants, practisers of witchcraft, the mentally unwell and an increasing pack of wild dogs.

"We call it the Tower of Terror," Neil says, "Many call it the Ghost Tower. Either name is apt as it's as if there's a haunting of some sort on each floor.

"The most recent death occurred on the 43rd floor. They found a Swedish backpacker hanging in one of the bathrooms. It smells forever musty up there, but this particular day there was an overwhelming, rancid stench of death. A photographer was climbing the tower to photograph the sunrise, when he was overcome by this ghastly smell as he reached the 43rd floor.

"He wandered the dimly-lit corridors, treading gingerly over the endless piles of debris that litter the place and came face to face with the terrifying sight of the backpacker hanging in a shower cubicle.

"They say the backpacker's ghost has been seen on several occasions. He has suddenly appeared out of the darkness, telling some totally stunned onlookers that he has to go and take a shower."

Despite being officially off-limits to the public, it is understood the number of people entering the Tower of Terror illegally has increased with over a hundred entering on any given weekend.

"It's pretty well understood that the security guards are easily bribed," Neil says. "Often the guards are happy for the visitors as they don't like to be wandering the building alone when it is so obviously haunted."

Adding weight to the haunted theory is the fact the building was constructed over a former cemetery.

While the skyscraper's 43rd floor is the most visited, and according to vigilant ghost watchers, the floor with the most recorded paranormal activity, the scariest floor is Number 19.

Eyewitnesses maintain a woman, known as the Death Witch, a hideous, slumped Chinese woman leaning on a wooden staff, her movement hindered by a twisted left leg, appears by the dust-

covered windows. She is said to beckon people to the window and as they approach she uses mental telepathy to fill their minds with thoughts of jumping.

Many have managed to run from her but up to seven people have been reported to have jumped to their deaths, lured to their doom by the insistent beckonings of the Death Witch."

The pack of wild dogs, who now run amok over several floors, are heard to start barking uncontrollably whenever they prowl Floor 19. Many believe they are barking at the Death Witch.

Local residents also say the Tower Of Terror is its liveliest at night. Many have filed complaints about the increased level of noise coming from the Tower at nightfall.

"If it's not the dogs barking, it's the screams of people falling to their death having been lured to the edge by the Death Witch," Neil says.

The building is also said to be a meeting place for drug dealers. Throughout the years, bodies have been discovered on various floors. Many of the dead have overdosed, while others have been viciously murdered – the price they pay for doing business with the unseemly world of the Asian drug lords.

"Some people, innocently exploring the building looking for ghosts, have accidently stumbled on a drug deal and have paid the ultimate price for seeing too much," Neil says, his face drained of its normal trademark smile. "You have to remember it is a dark and haunted place and attracts a fair share of the wrong type.

"As if the ghosts aren't scary enough, you can come face to face with some pretty evil people. And the narrow stairwell, laden with discarded building materials and the detritus of sexual dalliances, is incredibly claustrophobic. There's only a few light bulbs casting an eerie yellow glow; some floors have no light at all and you have to make your way up the stairs in complete pitch darkness.

"Sometimes as we gingerly walk through the dark you will feel a ghostly hand that you can't see pull at your hair or slap you hard across the face. It's terrifying."

But Neil says the heart-stopping, haunted walk is worth all the hair-raising terror with the reward of that breathtaking view that meets you on Level 49.

"You can't beat it," he says, his smile returning. "Suddenly confronted with that view, you forget about the dead bodies you may have stepped over to reach the top. You forget about the Death Witch and the hanging backpacker. It may take you 30 minutes to reach the top, but those panoramic views over Bangkok's urban skyline knock you for six. There's nothing like it.

"The only problem is, once you've taken in the wonder of that view, you then have to make the terrifying trek back down through darkness. And like I said, you never know who or what may be waiting for you around the corner on the next floor.

"The view is great, but it really is a haunted skyscraper. A true tower of terror."

* * *

THE GHOSTS OF THE TITANIC

There's an old leather shoe nestled in silt at the bottom of the Atlantic Ocean. It's rested there since April 15, 1912. It lingers alongside other people's belongings, right near the colossal wreck of the great Titanic.

The shoe, now non-descript in color, was once worn by a fireman, or stoker.

He would have been a brawny man, one of 150 whose thankless job it was to stand before ferocious furnaces relentlessly shoveling coal – feeding the flames to keep the Titanic's boilers steaming and the ship at the right speed.

Australian Andrew Rogers can't get the image of the shoe out of his head. He's been haunted by it since he first laid eyes on it in September 1998.

Andrew, then 34, had won a trip to be one of the first in the world, outside of the scientific community, to venture in a cramped submarine to the bottom of the North Atlantic to see first-hand the wreck of the most famous ship in the world: RMS Titanic. It would prove to be a life-changing trip and see the laid-back Aussie greenkeeper helping to lay one of Titanic's many ghosts finally to rest.

"Suddenly I'm 600 kilometers off the coast of Newfoundland in Canada aboard the research ship Akademik Keldysh, climbing into a submersible pod, the Mir 2, about to go and see something I've been reading about and hearing about all my life," Andrew says, shaking his head. "It's still very surreal."

He remembers the descent, mostly in complete darkness that took a staggering two hours.

"At about 100 meters, the light vanishes. It suddenly goes pitch black and we still had an hour and three quarters until we reached the bottom," he recalls. "There was a lot of time to think about things. I remember thinking about what happened on that fateful night and here I was sinking down too, in the same waters, exactly where it happened. It was phenomenal just how deep the ocean is and how dark it is – it's too hard to comprehend.

"My mind was racing to what those poor people aboard would have been thinking at the time, knowing they were all going to die. You can't imagine what that would feel like. Well, sadly they would have all been dead by that time. The horror of it all – people being stuck in it and getting sucked down with the ship."

Suddenly the lights were turned on and Andrew pushed his face up against one of the sub's thick windows. He admits that what he saw completely overwhelmed him. There he was, face to face with the skeletal remains of the Titanic.

"It was just eerie," he says. "I'm not going to overuse the word too much, but it was eerie. There were three of us there in the submersible, each of us consumed by what we could see through our portholes. There was complete silence just the whirring of the sub's engine. We were lost in wonder, looking out to where the light was shining on things that have been mostly in darkness for over 100 years.

"I tell you, it felt like we were in another world. It felt like we had gone into outer space then suddenly we were confronted joltingly with things manmade. That was the thrill – it took me about a half hour to get over that moment, I think."

The three adventurers spent more than five hours surreally touring the wreck. It was the ultimate underwater magic carpet ride.

"I could see the bridge, officers' quarters and passengers' cabins and windows. We hovered over toilets, bed pans, wash basins, plates, cups, tea pots, shoes, suitcases, a bathtub – all just there sitting on the silty bottom of the ocean. We went inside the wreck and went down the grand staircase that you see featured in the movie Titanic. It was truly heart-stopping. The chandeliers were still attached to the ceiling."

Andrew says the whole time everything was reminding him of the people. Those people, now ghostly and long gone, only their possessions at swim on the bottom of the Atlantic.

"I was transfixed by the shoe," he says. "I knew from my reading that it was a stoker's shoe. I tried to imagine his life. That's what made it so eerie; we were looking at things that belonged to real people. Seeing these tangible objects, you start imagining things in your head. I pictured the people panicking, people like the stoker working, people trying to stay calm. The people who stayed calm are probably the ones who went down with the ship to become lost souls.

"Honestly, I knew we were gazing upon what would be the most famous graveyard in the world."

Approximately 1,500 people lost their lives that night in the most horrific of circumstances. Asked if he believes, like so many do, that such a traumatic and emotional event would leave behind ghosts and make the site of the wreck and its strewn artifacts a haunted place, Andrew falls silent.

"I say it's haunting," he says, pensively. "It really hit me later that evening when I was back in my cabin. I was staring out into the blackness of the open ocean. I imagined being out there floating in the water, with no one to come and rescue me. I couldn't quite grasp everything I'd seen that day. I had a sad, eerie feeling. What I experienced – it certainly stayed with me."

Indeed it did. Back home in Australia, Andrew began researching the lives of five Australians known to have been on board. Then to his delight, he discovered there was a sixth, Evelyn Marsden, and she had survived.

"Evelyn is my favorite story," he says, smiling. "She was 32 and had signed on with the crew as a nurse and stewardess. She was lucky enough to escape the sinking by getting lifeboat number 16.

"She survived the sinking, went back to Southampton and married a Welsh Doctor, William Abel James. They ended up moving to Australia and finished up living in Bondi. They both died in 1938 in their 50s."

Andrew wondered where Evelyn was buried.

"I wanted to go and pay my respects and find out more about Evelyn," he says. "I imagined she would have a big headstone detailing her incredible story."

Through various records, he was able to locate Evelyn's grave in Sydney's Waverly Cemetery.

"It was sad when I located her grave. It was a single grave with two people in it and no tombstone at all. See, they had no children there were no relatives in Australia, so they just dug a hole and put her in it. Sadly, her husband died a week later from a broken heart. He committed suicide.

"If Evelyn were around today and survived such a high profile, tragic disaster, she would have been feted by every media company all around the world.

"But she didn't make a fuss, she just came home and got on with her life.

"The records showed she had died from bronchial pneumonia. I was so sad to find this lady with such an amazing story had not even a tombstone to remember her by."

By this stage, Andrew was making a name for himself as a Titanic aficionado, appearing on TV chat shows with his amazing footage from the wreck. He was appearing in schools' education programs and giving talks to community groups and maritime museums around Australia.

He shared his story about Evelyn with Australian journalist Lisa Wilkinson who, at the time, was the Editor-At-Large with national magazine *The Australian Women's Weekly*, and the magazine jumped at the chance to fund the tombstone.

"I was thrilled for Evelyn," he says proudly. "It just wasn't right her lying there in an unmarked grave and no one knowing her amazing story. Lying in an unmarked grave, she may as well have been lost at sea like the stoker and his shoe. I'm really proud of the tombstone, it gives her an identity. I really felt like I was helping to properly put her to rest."

* * *

THE GHOST NURSE OF THE JUAREZ HOSPITAL, MEXICO

If you fall ill in the crowded streets of Mexico City, there's every chance the ambulance will deliver you to Juarez Hospital.

Located in the Historical Centre between the teeming boulevards of Jose Maria and Fray Servando, Juarez has long been a beacon for those in need of high-quality medical attention.

Here you will be in the best of care, and if you find yourself being tended to by seemingly ethereal hands, it may just well be a very special nurse has come calling for you.

Pristine and dressed in any number of whiter-than-white nurses' uniforms from the 1930s to the 60s and right up until the present, this highly starched, perfectly ironed vision is known as La Planchada – it's Spanish for "the Ironed Lady." She has been seen by too many for her not to be real.

From seemingly nowhere she appears in the corridors of Juarez Hospital, usually in the Emergency wards, wanting to heal the sick.

There are different accounts about her appearance. Some say she glows, others that she looks just like a normal nurse. There have been some (often not believed) who say she floats up the corridors. Then others claim she walks but her footsteps never make a sound.

Either way, this nurse is always on night duty. She has never been seen in the light of day. Those who claim to have seen her have woken up the next day magically feeling better and found themselves transferred from the Emergency and Palliative sections of the hospital back to the géneral wards.

When asked why they have made such a seemingly quick and miraculous recovery, the answer has always been consistent, "The beautiful nurse, so white and well-ironed, came in and laid hands on me and told me I was healed," or words to that effect. Many of the medical staff look at the medical charts and claim there was no such nurse on duty that night. But some nod knowingly and simply say, "Ah! You had a visit from La Planchada! No wonder you're recovering so quickly!"

So who is, or was La Planchada?

Eulalia was a young, enthusiastic nurse of exceptional talent, care and empathy for the sick and poor. She joined the Juarez Hospital in the 1930s and the medical staff loved her for her exceptional dedication to helping the sick. She was respectful to the medical staff and playful and loving and immensely gentle when it came to the patients. Many thought her zeal went beyond the call of duty.

Her white uniform was never creased; it was as if she carried an iron with her to ensure there was never the sign of a wrinkle.

But then a handsome young doctor, Dr Joaquin, joined the hospital. While all the other nurses flirted with Dr Joaquin, Eulalia would always resist, never wanting to compromise the high standard of care she brought to her patients. She staunchly believed that romance between a doctor and a nurse was a no-no.

Dr Joaquin was a master of charm and a master in the operating theatre. It was one day whilst he was removing a bullet with his immaculate hands and deft surgical skills that Eulalia fell under his spell. They fell hopelessly in love and soon were happy to tell hospital staff and patients they were engaged to be married.

In the days leading up to their wedding, Joaquin was summoned to attend a medical seminar out of town. He came to Eulalia asking her to iron and press beautifully his suit, just the same way she did all her immaculate uniforms. Eulalia happily obliged. She poured her heart and soul into the ironing of her future husband's suit.

Joaquin was meant to be gone only 15 days. When day 18 arrived and he was still not back, Eulalia was beside herself with worry. Another week passed and the hospital got word that Dr Joaquin was on his honeymoon and he would not be returning to Eulalia or the hospital.

Eulalia couldn't believe such treachery. Could the man she gave her heart to – and indeed was going to marry – really be that cruel? She realized then he had actually asked her to press and iron his

Wedding Suit. A suit he would happily wear while marrying another.

Eulalia became mad with depression. Consumed with sorrow, she started to appear disheveled. The high standard of her work also suffered. Her patients started to be neglected and sadly due to her lack of vigilance, one died. She knew it was her fault.

The once brilliantly gifted and immaculate nurse was now a shadow of her former self and soon became a patient at the hospital where she once worked and shone. She lost the will to live and died.

Not long after her tragic passing, a beautiful new nurse was seen along the Emergency Wards. She was seen by doctors, nurses and patients. It is believed this was the ghost of Eulalia returning as a spirit nurse, ravaged with guilt by her neglect of duty of care. Many say that poor Eulalia can't pass over and is doomed to pay for her mistake for eternity. In death, she has returned to the immaculate, neatly-ironed, dedicated nurse she once was.

Chillingly, she is regularly seen tending to whatever patient is in the ward where she died. Each account consistently says this beautiful nurse was immaculate and her uniform was whiter than white and perfectly pressed.

Further to the ongoing presence of La Planchada making the Juarez Hospital a haunted place, the tragedy and miracles that came from the 1985 Mexico City earthquake have further cemented its position.

On the morning of Thursday, 19 September, the violent quake struck Great Mexico city leaving up to 40,000 dead or unaccounted for.

The 12-story-high Juarez Hospital was 80% full. It was shift change time when the quake struck. Within minutes the hospital collapsed, crushing and trapping countless people in the rubble.

Something wonderful happened in the midst of the devastating tragedy. Something unquestionably supernatural and miraculous. Nearly all the newborn babies in the nursery at the time of the quake were pulled out alive. Sadly, all their mothers did not survive. What made their rescue more amazing – what would go on to be called the "Miracle of Hospital Juarez" – was that these babies had been strewn amongst the devastation of the collapsed building for a staggering seven days before they were found and rescued.

These miracle babies had survived that length of time without the nourishment of their mothers' breast milk, water, warmth or human contact.

Or had a mystery nurse, La Planchada, reached them and cared for them until their rescuers came. Many say it was a miracle of God, many believe La Planchada played her part. Most believe it was both.

THE LIME TREE HOTEL, BORNEO

Terrified by her haunted Borneo Bathroom

Every time Ciara Rogers has to turn on the shower, she gets a bit goose bumpy, her body gives an involuntary shiver.

For the turning on of taps transports her straight back to a hotel room in Borneo and its bathroom constantly occupied by a sinister poltergeist.

"We were staying at the Lime Tree Hotel, in Kuching, Surowac," Ciara, then a Year 11 student at Stella Maris Catholic Girls High School in Manly, Australia, recalls. "I was there with some fellow students and teachers and we were in the middle of the Duke of Edinburgh Gold Trip."

The group were all excited about their upcoming Borneo adventure the afternoon they checked into the Lime Tree on the afternoon of October 4, 2016. But the mood soon shifted down to a low gear when Ciara and her two friends, Millie Jones and Georgia Mayer, entered their allocated apartment, Room 208.

"None of us said anything at first," Ciara recalls. "But all three of us would later admit we felt something sinister the moment we turned the key and opened the door. Each of us had a gut feeling something bad was in our room. Honestly, from the moment we entered we were overcome with a sense of worry and this unexplained weird feeling."

All the other students had been divided up into groups of two. Because Ciara was in a group of three, they were given the bigger room and thus their room became the fun meeting place for all the other students to gather.

"Everyone came to our room that first night and we were all in high spirits, chatting and laughing," Ciara says. "Then suddenly another of our friends, Ali, suddenly said, 'I reckon this room is haunted. No seriously, there is something not quite right here.'"

Most of the girls started laughing, some screamed for fun, but I remember looking at Millie and Georgia and for the first time we acknowledged it too.

"'I felt something the moment we walked in,'" Millie said while Georgia and I nodded in full agreement. I then said, 'I didn't want to say anything because I didn't want us all to be terrified.

"We all giggled and tried to make light of it, but that night I lay awake and I could hear the gurgling of the drain coming from the bathroom. It made an echoing, windswept whooshing noise, the same sort of sound you hear when you press your ear to a shell. But amid the sounds of the sea I could hear whispers, pleading whispers and screams, then a shocking choking noise. I put my pillow to my ears to block out the tormenting noise of sea mingling with screams and whispers."

But the first night was only a taste of the terror that was to come with the setting of the sun on the second night.

"That night, Millie was first to have a shower. We all thought the bathroom with its whispering drains was creepy so we were all a bit scared to go in there.

"Millie was at the tail end of her shower when she saw the toilet roll starting to unravel. There were no air vents in the bathroom, the window wasn't open. There was nothing to create a breeze that would have shifted the toilet roll.

"At first it started unraveling slowly, then it started to spin faster and faster. Millie came running terrified with her towel hurriedly wrapped around her.

"'Guys,' she screamed, pointing in at the toilet. 'Look!' We all saw it and stared with total disbelief. The toilet roll was unraveling at great speed, the paper cascading in torrents over the wet bathroom floor. It was so creepy and Georgia and I were yet to have our showers!

"I'm quite a hygiene freak and I was determined nothing was going to stop me from taking my shower."

Gingerly, Ciara entered the bathroom with the promise her girlfriends would be right outside the door should something sinister occur.

Above from the left: Millie Jones, Georgia Mayer and Ciara Rogers

"I was totally creeped out and terrified," Ciara says. "I told the girls 'I am going to yell out the moment something happens. I can't believe I'm risking my life to take a shower!'

"I was so scared, I was trying so hard not to close my eyes when I was shampooing my hair. I wanted to see if anything was happening."

Ciara was relieved once she was clean and her hair had been rinsed of shampoo free of any spooky incident. But her peace was short lived.

"I turned the shower off, grabbed my towel, and as I was stepping from the cubicle, the douche that hung on a hook next to the toilet cistern came flying off the hook, lunging at me as you see a cobra lunging at a snake charmer.

"I came running out of the bathroom and the girls saw the douche flying through the air. I was scared and dripping and barely able to breathe. There was no explanation as to why the douche and its long hose would fly through the air like that.

"We stared back into the room with total disbelief. A brave Georgia picked up the douche and returned it to its hook. She was brave enough to go into the bathroom and do that, but she maintained there was no way she going in there to take a shower."

The girls were too scared to go to bed and turn out the lights. They huddled together and tried to make sense of the spinning, cascading, out-of-control toilet roll and the mysterious levitating douche.

"But how could we make sense of any of it," Ciara says. "We stayed up for hours, terrified beyond words. We were exhausted, but too scared to go to bed and close our eyes.

"We pushed all our beds together, then closed the bathroom door and prayed nothing else would happen. We couldn't wait for morning to come.

"We kept the bedside lights on, and tried so hard to stay awake. Somehow we all managed to finally drift off."

The next day the girls told their friends and teachers of the horrors of their Borneo Bathroom.

"No one doubted what we'd experienced. Someone said these exotic places are often rife with sprits and poltergeists.

"The hotel staff just smiled knowingly when we told them we thought there was a ghost in Room 208.

"I am convinced we encountered something bad in that bathroom. There was a haunted presence and it didn't give us a good feeling.

"I remember looking back into the bathroom on the morning we were checking out. The drain was beckoning with its screams and mysterious whispers. I shuddered, picked up my bag and scurried out as fast as I could.

"The memory still haunts us and we often recall the haunted Borneo Bathroom. There is no way I will ever go back to stay at The Lime Tree Hotel."

* * *

THE MANCHAC WETLANDS, UNITED STATES

Just a few miles down the road from New Orleans, the air turns thick with swamp mist. There's a point along this darkened stretch of road where the echoing wails from jazz joints suddenly fall silent, the neon lights that glisten off the clouds above Bourbon Street fade. The only light to be found: the sudden flash of a firefly darting through a twisted clutch of grey cypress.

Welcome to Manchac Swamp. Here the muddy waters are thick and dormant – the color, a sickly green like rancid pea soup. Venture in a ways, your tin boat bumping over logs or perhaps the gnarled heads of crocodiles, and you are sure to bump up against a stumpy old shack. The shack belonged to legendary voodoo queen, Julia Brown.

She was known to all around the swamplands for her Voodoo ways. She'd sit on her porch making up charms and love potions and spitting out curses. Most the folk around New Orleans, and Frenier, the town at the edge of the swamp, were terrified of Julia Brown.

Some called her Julia Black, others White, depending on her many shifting moods. Some days she was all sweet talcum and white lace, holding court while singing gently and making love potions and good luck charms to assuage the lonely and those fallen on hard times. These were her "White" days. Other times, her "Black" days, Julia would be fired up with a vengeful, hate-filled temper, concocting needle-stabbed Voodoo Dolls, spitting and hollering curses across the muddy waters of the swamp.

On these days, the poor cabbage farmers who eked out their existence around the swamp would look up in disgust and horror. They'd fend off the glaring intensity of the sun with the back of their hands, to squint and stare in the direction of Julia's menacing porch.

"She's at it again," they'd say in whispered, knowing tones.

"Someone's going to die – you can feel it."

One quiet evening, Julia, smoking a pipe, adorned in flowing robes and clanging bangles, sat upon her porch and stared into the swamp. It was one of those nights where folk, faded from a working day of heat, would just sit and languish on stoops and porches, fan themselves and wish they could cool themselves with a dip in deep swamp water. The alligators made sure swimming wasn't a Louisiana past time.

This night, Julia began singing for her heatstroke-ravaged audience. "One day I'm gonna die," she sang. "And I'm gonna take all of you with me."

Porch swings banged against yellowing weather boards. Disgusted folk, a mixture of reverent fear and downright anger, took their leave and went indoors. Julia stayed on her porch swing singing curses aimed at her neighbors.

Her words, as many there on the night feared, proved to be prophetic.

Night after night, for the next few weeks, Julia would appear and sing her cursed song into the night. She sang it one last time before she fell down dead.

On September 29, 1915, the day of her funeral, a cyclone with all the fury of Julia's black temper came seemingly out of nowhere.

No sooner were the nails hammered into her coffin, the prophecy of Julia was unleashed. The entire town, wanting to make peace with the fearful black witch, had gathered for her funeral. The cyclone wiped out three towns and saved its most destructive belt for the mourners at Julia's grave. Only two citizens survived the wrath of Julia Brown's curse.

Close to 300 people in Louisiana died that day. Houses were flattened, rows of shops blown away and miles of railway tracks washed to a swampy oblivion. One of the only survivors later said he'd clung to an upturned cypress tree and tried to block his ears against the terrified screams of those drowning in the swamp.

One local newspaper, the *New Orleans Times-Picayune*, on October 2, 1915 reported on The Voodoo Queen's bizarre and terrifying funeral:

"Many pranks were played by wind and tide. Negroes had

gathered for miles around to attend the funeral of 'Aunt' Julia Brown, an old negress who was well known in that section, and was a big property owner. The funeral was scheduled … and 'Aunt' Julia had been placed in her casket and the casket in turn had been placed in the customary wooden box and sealed. At 4 o'clock, however, the storm had become so violent that the negroes left the house in a stampede, abandoning the corpse. The corpse was found Thursday and so was the wooden box, but the casket never has been found."

It's little wonder that today locals and paranormal experts are unified in declaring Manchac Swamp and its nearby surrounds a haunted place. They say the place has more ghosts than mosquitos.

So many people drowned in Julia's Cursed Cyclone that locals maintain it's quite common for skeletons to still surface today.

The swamp is now a bird sanctuary. By day it looks to be one of the most tranquil and serene of places – a haven for the wonders of nature. But at night, when mosquitos blanket the rancid waters and fireflies offer only the faintest glimpses of light, the swamp takes on its sinister, voodoo-cursed identity. Those who like the dark arts are said to flock to the swamp come nightfall in the hope of conjuring the ghost of the Voodoo Queen. The wide-eyed, ghost-tour enthusiasts wanting a laugh and a good scare also come to the swamp at night. Some get more than they bargain for with the odd sighting of a floating skeleton.

Black or White, there is no question the ghost of Julia Brown the Voodoo Queen now reigns over the countless souls who perished in the murderous storm of her making.

Many have claimed to have seen her cackling maniacally from the porch of her now-dilapidated cabin. Others swear they have heard her haunting voice singing that dreadful cursed song – the lyrics of promised doom and misery, ringing across the turbid waters of the swamp.

* * *

THE MOORS MURDERS, UNITED KINGDOM

Until the body of missing teenager Keith Bennett has been found and put to rest, the Moors Murders will continue to haunt and torment.

And the place where these horrific crimes were carried out – Saddleworth Moor, will always be known as a place of unspeakable horror, torment and terror and will forever be haunted.

Since the 60s, many a nightmare has been had over the horror that is the Moors Murders. The names Ian Brady and Myra Hindley conjuring instant terror, often nausea – this twisted, sadistic couple, the epitome of evil.

Between 1963 and 1965, they murdered five innocent and very trusting children aged between 10 and 17. Pauline Reade, John Kilbride, Keith Bennett, Lesley Ann Downey and Edward Evans, were all unfortunate to cross the paths of Brady and Hindley.

The victims were abducted raped, tortured then murdered. Some of the murders took place within Brady's and Hindley's squalid homes or out on windswept and remote Saddleworth Moor. Three of their victims were buried out on the Moors. A fourth victim, Keith Bennett, is also suspected to be buried out there, but his body has never been found.

It was the killing of Edward Evans, 17, that brought them undone. They had lured the boy to their house and a crazed Brady bludgeoned him with an axe while Myra's brother-in-law David Smith was visiting.

Brady must have thought Smith would be impressed by the crazed slaughter. He couldn't have been more wrong. A terrified Smith went to the police. He also informed the police that Brady had boasted of killing other children and burying them out on Saddleworth Moor. The police swooped.

Brady and Hindley had spent "happy days" out on the Moor. They'd picnic and take photos of each other – often posing happily on the graves of their victims. To the unknowing, the photos are of a carefree couple in love. It's hard to believe that just hours before the various photos were posed for and taken – both had engaged in prolonged acts of sexual torture on children, culminating in their murders.

The photos are of a couple cavorting and celebrating love – when in reality they were celebrating their evil. Clearly, from the happiness displayed in these photos – there was not a second of regret, guilt or remorse.

These photos would also bring them unstuck when discovered by police.

In October 1965, the naked body of Lesley Ann Downey was discovered on the Moors. John Kilbride's body was discovered 11 days later.

The discovery of the bodies, was largely helped by the "trophy" photos of Brady and Hindley proudly smiling at the scene.

Despite two bodies being discovered on the Moors, the police knew they only had circumstantial evidence against Hindley and Brady. But when they re-searched their house, they found a luggage ticket which led them to a locker at Manchester's Central Station.

Inside the locker were sadistic gadgets and pornography including horrific photos of little Lesley Ann, bound and gagged in Hindley's bedroom. And then there was the tape recording of Lesley's sexual torture and murder. The little, terrified girl can be heard politely begging for her life, then there is crying and screaming and the angry voices of Hindley and Brady mocking her and yelling over her while demanding she do things that were obviously causing her to recoil in agony.

When the tape was played in court, the true evil and merciless sadism of the pair was revealed to the world.

Myra Hindley, named by the British Press as "the most evil woman in Britain", will be forever etched in our minds in a black and white 1960s mug shot, her bleached hair teased and bouffant, her eyes blackened and leering.

The fact that a woman, who is meant to be naturally maternal, could have participated in such horrendous crimes against children – seemed to make her the focal point of the Moors Murders. This despite it being the psychotic Brady with his love of Nazism and animal torture and the belief that "rape and murder are good", who was the mastermind behind the sickening atrocities.

Brady and Hindley were convicted of murdering Lesley Ann Downey and Edward Evans. Brady was also convicted of the murder of John Kilbride. They were both sentenced to life in prison.

At the time of their sentencing, they were both strongly suspected of being responsible for the disappearance and murders of Keith Bennett and Pauline Reade, but their bodies had not been found at the time of the trial.

Years later, in the 1980s the pair finally confessed to the killings. They were both taken back to Saddleworth Moor, to help police find the graves of the missing children.

It took months of digging, but police finally were able to locate the mummified remains of Pauline Reade.

Tragically, 12-year-old Keith Bennett's body has never been found. His grief-stricken mum, Winnie spent almost fifty years tormented and searching for her son. Sadly, the 78-year-old died in 2012 without fulfilling her lifelong wish to find her son's makeshift grave on Saddleworth Moor and give him a proper Christian burial. She even begged Brady to help and, right to the end, a callous Brady played with her.

As one police officer said at the time: "In the end one man holds the key to where Keith Bennett's body is. One act of humanity would help Winnie find some peace."

Brady, sadistic even in old age, smirked and refused to help.

Hindley died in prison in 2002, aged 60. She died as the most despised woman in Britain. So much so that 20 local undertakers refused to take her body, claiming that she was too bad to bury and she will never be at rest or at peace.

She was finally accepted for cremation, but as for her ashes – no one knows.

Many believe her ghost has returned to Saddleworth Moor, cementing the location as a haunted place, dripping evil. Her ghost is said to be wandering among her killing fields, many believe she will stop the body of Keith Bennett ever being found and finally laid to rest.

The singer Morrissey, renowned for his dark songs, has no doubt

Saddleworth Moor is haunted. The former Smiths singer believes he encountered the ghost of a troubled young man – naked apart from an anorak when he drove through the area with friends in 1989.

Morrissey was terrified by the encounter.

He described Saddleworth Moor as "the most barren, desolate, desperate place".

He said of the ghost: "He just emerged from the heather and pleaded to the lights, and we drove past because we all instinctively knew this was a spirit and because it had a history of being a place where so many bodies have been dumped and buried. It's not really the kind of place you hang around.

"We went to the phone box in the nearest village and called the police.

"We said, 'We have just driven down the Wessenden Road on Saddleworth Moor, and somebody has emerged from the side of the road and pleaded to the car.' The police said, 'Keep an open mind.'"

The next day Morrissey returned to the same spot to find it totally deserted with no buildings or pathways within sight. He was completely flummoxed.

Could he have possibly encountered the ghost Keith Bennett?

"Was it somebody who was being chased? Or was it the spectre of somebody who had been dumped on the moors many years ago?

"This person was not human, and it was very, very frightening."

This ghostly encounter was made more chilling and poignant because Morrissey has long been vocal about the deep impression left on him by the Moors Murders as a child.

The Smiths' first song, *Suffer Little Children*, was written about the killing by Ian Brady and Myra Hindley.

Morrissey's encounter with the spectre has left little doubt that Saddleworth Moor will continue to be a haunted place.

It is probable the tormented ghost of Myra Hindley will ensure it will forever stay that way. Meanwhile, people still hold out hope that the Moors will reveal its final secret and allow Keith Bennett's remains to be found so he can be put to rest alongside his long-suffering mum. Both of them finding peace, at last!

* * *

THE MYSTERIOUS FRAULEIN
OF THE ROSENSTEIN RUINS, GERMANY

Be careful as you go treading gingerly into the ruins of the Rosenstein Castle.

The history books tell us Rosenstein Castle first came into being around 1282. Following a series of wars, and various Counts and Barons owning the imposing mountain top wonder, the castle was left to sit silent and alone. It has been this way, slowly crumbling and disappearing into Mount Rosenstein upon which it was built since 1524. Only 48 years after its abandonment, the castle was already being listed officially on local maps as a "ruin."

The centuries have come and gone, but interest in this Medieval landmark, offering magnificent views over the town of Heubach, has never ceased to wane.

Most make the beautiful hike up the mountain from Heubach to drink in that view. Others come foolishly tempting fate, hopeful of a possible run-in with the castle's legendary ghost: the Rosenstein Fraulein.

So who is this restless soul left to wander the castle's windswept ruins for close to half a century? She is barely able to be found in the official annals of history, but folklore and rumor have kept her spectral image glowing brightly atop that mountain.

Graham O'Donoghoe, an acclaimed pastry chef hailing from the Northern Beaches of Sydney Australia, recalls his time in Heubach in the early 1980s.

"I was in Germany studying to be a pastry chef," Graham says. "I was young, in my late teens, in a new country and open to all the fun and endless possibilities on offer to free-spirited teenagers.

"One night I was seated in a pub with my new German friends,

many of them Heubach locals, and they began telling me to be careful of the Rosenstein Fraulein. They spoke of her in revered and hushed tones.

"I'd been telling my friends that I planned to hike up to the castle ruins the next day and I asked if any of them would like to come. They looked at me as if I were mad. Some laughed and cajoled each other into telling me about the Rosenstein Fraulein."

Graham was all ears as he was regaled with stories of the mysterious woman.

"'If you must go, you should be very careful, and don't do anything to invoke the wrath of the Rosenstein Fraulein,' one warned me. 'Never, ever go up to the ruins, as other children from our village have, and call out "Rosenstein Fraulein, ich verfluche (I curse you)."' I could feel my skin going cold.

"I was told that if I dared to say that three times in a row, peril would rain down upon me and it was highly likely I would plunge off the mountain. 'Many have, they told me. Others have been tormented to death, hearing the screams of the deranged Fraulein.'"

Graham left the pub glowing from the beers and his head swimming with the taunting phrase, 'Rosenstein Fraulein, ich verfluche!' He imagined he'd see the mysterious woman, robes billowing beneath a crumbling stone archway.

"In my mind, I thought the woman would be ethereal and haunted, looking like Kate Bush in the Wuthering Heights film clip," Graham laughs. "I remember singing Wuthering Heights as I began the leisurely hike winding from Heubach up into the leafy Rosenstein Mountain the next day."

Graham had been told various stories regarding the woman who became the ghost of the mountain. Some said she was the mistress of the last occupant of the castle, Georg von Woellwarth. She was spurned by the wealthy baron and chained to the castle walls, screaming and left to rot as he rode away to start a new life in the valley below.

Others claimed she was a servant who went mad, killed a child and jumped to her death from a castle window. Many who venture close to the castle ruins claim they can hear her screams as she plunges to her death.

"I'm sure I heard the screams," Graham says. "As silly as it sounds, I'm convinced I heard the screams. They terrified me. It would have been easy to dismiss them as my imagination playing tricks on me, I wanted to. But as I approached the ruins, they became so audible, I couldn't dismiss them as imagined or just the wind."

Staring back over Heubach, Graham felt elated by the view and was able to put the scary thoughts of the Fraulein to the back of his mind.

"I loved being up there," Graham says. "There was a Led Zeppelin album, Houses Of The Holy – the album cover could have been shot up there among the Medieval ruins. I started singing songs from that album and decided to wander through the many caves of the Rosenstein.

"There are about 40 caves up there. I imagined Miranda from *Picnic At Hanging Rock* wandering all distant and mysterious up there, being called back by her terrified classmates as she headed into forbidden places.

"It was then I got a bit of Dutch courage and decided to call out

'Rosenestein Fraulein, ich verfluche!' I could feel my heart rate racing as I made the third and final call. My call echoed, scarily bouncing off the cave walls. Nothing happened, and I laughed out loud trying to convince myself I wasn't scared, that I hadn't unleashed anything bad.

"But I was wrong, I could hear the screams again, this time louder and closer to me than before. I hit my head on a low-hanging rock as I tried to run from the cave. Holding my head, I then stumbled awkwardly and twisted my ankle. All the while the screaming, like the most vicious of winds, was bearing down on me. The screams were demented and horrific and furious – a similar sound to pterodactyls that you see in bad horror movies. It was interesting to learn later they found fossils of pterodactyls in the region.

"My head was hurting, the screams deafening, and my left ankle swelling. I could barely walk with it. I sort of scraped out of the cave rather than walked. Fittingly, the cave I fled from was called 'Sinister Hole'.

"I managed to stumble my way back to the picnic area and a lovely couple saw that I was shaken and in pain. 'Don't tell me, you upset the Fraulein,' the woman tutted knowingly as she handed me a glass of wine.

"Shamefaced, I confessed I had called out to her.

"The couple looked at each other, as if to say, 'another stupid tourist, tormenting that poor woman'.

"The kind couple drove me back to Heubach, and that night it was my turn to tell my friends ghost stories. They were wide-eyed with fright and all ears. None of them doubted what I'd experienced.

"All these decades later, I sometimes wake up sweating and able to hear the screaming. That awful screaming. I never actually saw the Rosenstein Fraulein. I know I heard her, and I know she's real. I should never have called her name."

* * *

THE QUEEN'S GHOSTLY GUESTS,
UNITED KINGDOM

The Queen is a firm believer in ghosts and she embraces the supernatural with great calmness and an unfazed acceptance.

Having spent her entire life residing in haunted royal residences, Her Majesty doesn't bat an eye or raise a goose bump when things go bump in the night.

In the early days of her reign, she famously dismissed a confronting ghostly visitation with the words, "Oh just another spook," before seamlessly getting on with what she does best – attending tirelessly to her royal duties.

She was a young princess when, along with little sister Princess Margaret, the Queen had her first ghostly encounter with what she firmly believes to be the ghost of Elizabeth I in the Green Drawing Room at Windsor Castle.

The Queen has since encountered her deceased namesake several times throughout her lengthy reign and smiles knowingly when she senses Elizabeth I's presence. In fact, the Queen is thrilled to have her deceased relative firmly ensconced in her favorite residence.

A courtier close to Her Majesty once revealed the entire Royal Family have no doubt that all the Queen's properties are haunted.

"They firmly believe in ghosts and often tell their alarmed guests that ghosts are present in all the royal homes," the courtier said. "The Royal Family, particularly the Queen, are not frightened of ghosts, they're just simply fascinated by them."

The ghost of Elizabeth I is just one of many specters said to walk the gilded floors of Windsor Castle. At last count, at least 25 spine-tingling spooks are said to waft merrily along the draughty, dimly-lit corridors.

Born in 1533, Elizabeth I was the only daughter of the fearsome

Henry VIII and Anne Boleyn. She died at age 69 in 1603 after reigning an impressive 45 years. Elizabeth I lived in terror of catching the plague, and had a gallows erected at Windsor Palace. Anyone suspected of carrying the disease was quickly rounded up and hanged without any questions being asked. Many of these hapless victims are said to be among the troubled ghosts at Windsor Castle.

The most fearsome of ghouls enjoying free reign wafting throughout Windsor Castle's 1,000 rooms is Herne the Hunter. Described in 14th Century record books as "a man clad in deer skins and a helmet from which issued magnificent antlers," Herne hung himself from an oak tree after being found guilty of poaching Henry VIII's deer. Other stories say he went insane after being wounded by a stag. He shed his clothes and ran for miles before hanging himself from an oak tree very close to the castle's wall. No matter which version of his demise you choose to believe, his restless, tormented spirit has been prowling the castle since. The last firm sighting was in 1976 by one of the Queen's Coldstream Guards.

Equally scary is the ghost of Henry VIII. Many have reported seeing him moaning and groaning loudly beneath the window where he first saw Anne Boleyn who he fell in love with, married, then later mercilessly had beheaded. Prince Charles has famously said he has seen the ghost of his infamous relative, describing him as "fat with a ginger beard."

King Henry VIII is responsible for many of the troubled souls haunting the Queen's many famous dwellings. His fifth wife, Catherine Howard, has haunted Hampton Court in West London for centuries.

Many claim to have heard her screams as she begged an unforgiving Henry VIII for mercy. Others have seen her running desperate and terrified through a gallery, her white face tormented with mental anguish.

Catherine was beheaded at the Tower of London for adultery with courtier Thomas Culpepper. While awaiting her grisly death sentence at Hampton Court, she escaped and ran along the gallery to hammer on Henry's door, desperately begging for mercy. Guards quickly set upon her and she was dragged away screaming in terror. She was executed on February 13, 1542 and her ghost returned to Hampton Court to wander tormented and never at peace.

The Queen's servants are often bemoaning the fact their places of work are quite terrifying thanks to the regular appearances of royal ghosts, something which her Majesty is said to find "jolly amusing."

In 1996, footman Shaun Croasdale ran screaming through the corridors of Sandringham House, the Queen's home in Norfolk, after seeing the ghost of Her Majesty's favorite servant who had died the previous year.

Shaun, 40 at the time, dropped several bottles of wine and fled in terror from the cellar after seeing the spirit of Tony Jarred, who passed away at 60 after 38 years of loyal service to the Royal Family.

Within minutes of hearing of Shaun's close encounter with Tony's ghost, the Queen summoned Shaun and insisted he tell her all about the experience. A trembling Shaun told the Queen how he turned round and saw Tony "as plain as daylight", dressed in the familiar blue apron he wore whilst working in the cellar. Shaun was so shaken that another member of staff had to fetch the day's drinks. It is understood the Queen ordered Shaun "a good stiff drink to steady you."

A courtier told the press, "The Queen was very fond of Tony and took comfort from the fact that he was still around. She believed every word of Shaun's story and there was never any question of his sanity being in doubt."

Sandringham has been the locale for several spirit sightings, making it one of the most actively haunted royal homes. Servants to the Queen have seen strange happenings in their rooms. Clothes and ornaments have suddenly moved around right before their very eyes. The Queen, whenever she hears of such unexplained occurrences, instantly wants to hear every single detail. When it comes to ghosts, she is a captive and enthusiastic audience.

But it's not only the servants telling ghostly tales. The Royal Family members themselves are quick to tell of their own supernatural run ins.

Prince Charles is forever recounting the time he and his then valet, Ken Stronach, entered the Library at Sandringham. The library is the oldest part of the palace.

"They felt very cold and were convinced someone was behind them," a courtier explains." But when they looked around, there was no one there. They looked at each other, uttered a nervous 'Oh, heck!' and ran. Charles still talks about it today; he was petrified."

The Queen Mum whilst still alive was often waxing lyrical about Glamis Castle, her childhood home in Scotland. The Castle is haunted by the sad "grey lady" – the beautiful Janet Douglas, Lady Glamis, who was burned at the stake in 1537 after being accused of witchcraft.

The Queen Mum said she sighted this tormented woman "many times" throughout the several years she resided at Glamis Castle. The Queen Mum also told of seeing the ghost of "the mad Earl of Glamis." The story goes that Lord and Lady Glamis had a hideously deformed son. He was covered in hair, had an egg-shaped head and was overwhelmingly strong. The Lord and Lady had their son locked away in a room high up in the castle and shamefully kept his existence a closely guarded secret.

The Queen Mum insisted she saw the ghost of this troubled and grotesque Earl haunting the castle. Other eyewitnesses supported her story by saying they had seen the same figure peering unhappily from the battlements and wandering along the roof.

A courtier ominously added weight to all the Royal hauntings by saying, "So many of us have seen ghosts, we all believe the royal homes are haunted. Sandringham has more than 270 rooms, but Windsor is the worst – parts are really scary," he said. "The Queen has never had them exorcised because she feels they add character and are harmless."

But there is one ghost The Queen does find troubling – the ethereal presence of the universally adored Diana, Princess of Wales.

Diana's ghost has been reportedly seen wandering sad and alone throughout the rooms of her former home, Kensington Palace. ·

Many staff have seen her – those Diana eyes – looking down over her beloved William and his treasured Kate and the grandchildren she never got to meet.

But the Queen won't discuss her thoughts on Diana's ghost, merely saying, "Diana is at peace."

Spoiled for choice when it comes to Royal ghosts, perhaps the Queen sees Diana as one ghost too many. Diana wanted to be remembered as the Queen of Hearts. Her Majesty will be known as the Queen of Haunted Places.

* * *

THE RED DUST GHOST OF COBAR, AUSTRALIA

You feel a chill the moment you climb the stairs to the Great Cobar Heritage Centre.

There's definitely a presence as you clutch the railing to marvel up at the impressive and imposing 1910 double-brick building that once served as the administrative office for the Great Cobar Copper Mine – at that time the largest copper mine in Australia.

Old buildings naturally conjure thoughts of ghostly faces at darkened windows. These thoughts are only heightened upon learning that there were160 recorded deaths during the heady days of the mine.

The place *must* be haunted!

It's a question tourism officer John Collins often ponders as he wanders the eerie corridors and abandoned mines surrounding the Heritage Centre in the north-western New South Wales outback town.

"I'm not a complete skeptic," John says as a lashing of red dust swirls up in the westerly wind and dances ghost-like before us. "I like to keep an open mind on things I don't understand. I believe the 'ghosts' are memories of the people who have lived, worked and died around the building."

And John is the first to admit there have been too many eerie sightings to be totally dismissive.

"It was only last year that a man who was in Cobar on council business, with no prior knowledge of Cobar or the building's history, came in to the museum one morning and asked me if anyone lived in the building," he says. "I told him, 'No, it's a museum, locked up with alarms set every night.' That's when he looked concerned. He told me that about 10 o'clock the previous night, he was jogging past the building and heard a girl screaming inside. His ashen face made me realize he definitely wasn't joking."

Other visitors have said that they felt unnerved as they wandered the site.

"Over the past seven years, I've had a number of people who claimed to be psychic come to me after walking through the museum and tell me there was significant 'activity' in certain rooms," John says. "And a previous curator had some professional psychics go over the place and they also said it was 'alive'."

The curator has also had his own freaky close-encounter with a ghost.

"Asleep one night in the building on his own, he claimed he was woken in the middle of the night when he felt a cold clammy hand gripping his foot," John says. "He ran out of the room screaming, and the story of Cobar's Miner's Ghost was born.

"The room where he had his experience was the pay office from the mining days. The story goes that it was a disgruntled miner who was owed money and fell and died in the Open Cut, a water-filled quarry next to the mine."

From that freaky encounter, Cobar's annual Miner's Ghost Festival was born and has been growing in popularity since 1998. It is held in late October.

But it is not only the miner's ghost lurking around the Heritage Centre. There is a cold presence in the makeshift mine beneath the center, and a wafting-white shadow that hovers near a vintage wicker pram... said to be a concerned mother watching over a sickly child.

Whether you believe in ghosts and haunted places, John says the festival is all about making merry.

"It's a great get together for locals and visitors alike. It's all about having fun, enjoying ourselves and reliving our mining heritage."

And the ghosts seem to be in high spirits too, no pun intended.

* * *

WAKEHURST PARKWAY GHOSTS, AUSTRALIA

Those who venture into the night to drive along the infamous stretch of bushland-shrouded road known as The Wakehurst Parkway seem to clutch their steering wheels in a firm, white-knuckled manner.

They lock their car doors, stare into the purple murk of the bitumen ahead of them and pray the drive will soon be over and their headlights will not shine upon anything foreboding.

For ghosts and The Wakehurst Parkway, a thoroughfare running through remote scrub at the back of Sydney's Northern Beaches, seem to go hand in hand. This lonely stretch of road is the stuff of legend.

Locals are all aware and speak in whispers about the forlorn girl in the white dress who steps out in front of cars, waves them down and asks to be driven home. As the obliging drivers approach the girl's requested destination, they turn to find their mystery passenger has vanished.

Then there is the phantom nun, serene and kind. She walks along the side of the road and good Samaritans stop to offer her a lift. No sooner is she in the car, her face turns to something horrific, eyewitnesses say "demonic", her voice changes, she screams with a wild fury, causing drivers to veer off the road and often crash. When they come to she is gone. While some say the nun is pure evil, others who have picked her up say she was nothing but serene. Many commenting on her piercing and intense green eyes that "shimmer like emeralds".

Ex cab driver Hla Oo described the nun on his blog: "There was a grey silhouette of a thin young woman in the mirror.

"She was in a kind of white gown and head-dress like a Christian nun.

"I couldn't really see her face clearly, just the shape of her face and her deep green eyes, yes the sad green eyes, but she was definitely real and sitting there and staring back at me at that precise moment."

Filmmaker Bianca Biasi found her drive along Wakehurst Parkway so intense she decided to turn it into a documentary, *The Parkway Hauntings*, where believers, skeptics and a medium investigate the paranormal goings on along the infamous stretch of road and the Deep Creek Reserve that runs off it.

The film takes believers and skeptics to the reserve with a spiritual medium to investigate reports of paranormal activity in the area.

Before long, believers and skeptics alike are falling ill and vomiting, sensing presences and refusing to return to the site.

"It was terrifying," says Bianca, who produced and co-directed *The Parkway Hauntings* at Deep Creek Reserve and has no doubt the area is haunted.

"I think I can safely say I don't ever want to go back to Deep Creek Reserve and I won't drive the Parkway again."

Northern Beaches mum, Jessica Crapis, 35, knows there "is something there", along the Wakehurst Parkway.

While Jessica has not encountered the girl in the white dress or the mysterious nun, she knows she came face to face with something so terrifying it left her comatose.

"I was going to visit a friend who was housesitting at Claireville," Jessica recalls. "My hubby was at home minding our two young children and I set off from Seaforth where we were living and started driving down the Wakehurst Parkway.

"I was so looking forward to seeing my friend. I drove along the first portion of the Parkway, crossed the intersection at Warringah Road and sailed down into the second section of the Parkway. It was the clearest of nights.

"As I drove deeper into the bush I noticed a cloud or a fog up ahead. It hovered right near where the C3 church is. This fog just appeared out of nowhere. Suddenly it was all around me. It was so thick I couldn't see."

Jessica slowed her car down and proceeded with caution. She couldn't see a thing and prayed another car wouldn't suddenly ram into the back of her.

"The last thing I remember is hoping if there was another car they would see me," Jessica recalls. "I drove through the lights near the C3 church and I blacked out.

"The next thing I recall is slowly coming to several minutes later and my hands were wrapped around the steering wheel so tightly that my arms were hurting. My mouth was wide open; I remember seeing it in the rear vision mirror. My mouth looked as if I were screaming in terror – but no sound was coming out."

Jessica has no idea what she encountered, what horror she saw that caused her to black out in the middle of a terrified, silent scream.

"I remember looking down at my hands clutching the wheel and they were white," she says. "It was as if the blood had drained from my body."

Jessica believes she encountered a ghost that day on the Wakehurst Parkway.

"Something happened out there on the road that night," she says, unable to explain exactly what. "It was weird. It was something supernatural – there is no other way to explain it.

"Why was the fog there? There was something there and it was trying to communicate with me. I think my blanking out was something protecting me from seeing something too horrible.

"I had heard all the stories about the Wakehurst Parkway and I know after my experience in the mystery fog – there is something going on along that road.

"I try not to drive down that way by myself. I never cease to get chills every time I drive past that spot. I know something happened there. I don't know what, but it definitely involved a haunting."

* * *

WAVERLY HILLS SANATORIUM, UNITED STATES

Located on a windswept hill in Louisville, Jefferson County, Kentucky, the Waverly Hills Sanatorium was built at a time when America was in the grips of the "white death" - otherwise known as tuberculosis (TB).

Louisville, situated on swampland, was the ultimate breeding ground for the disease and thus had one of the highest TB death rates in the United States.

The original wooden structured hospital, designed to specialize in fighting TB, was first built in 1910. But with the plague virtually out of control, a new hospital, the one we see today, opened in 1926.

Despite being regarded as the most advanced medical institution to fight tuberculosis, some 63,000 patients died there. Many succumbed to the ravages of the disease, others expired through mistreatment and as a result of barbaric and radical medical experiments.

Disease, mistreatment, questionable medical experiments – no wonder Waverly Hills, with such a sad and tragic past, has become one of the most haunted buildings in the USA.

Here, along its dimly lit corridors, past the abandoned nurses' stations, "treatment" rooms, clammy morgue, its glass-covered porches, empty stairwells – echo the voices of the dead. This once-stately building, eroding with time, is now the keeper of ghostly secrets and resident phantoms.

The curious, in their thousands, have flocked to Waverly Hills, hopeful of a close encounter. None, it seems, have left disappointed. So-called ghost researchers have left brimming with tales.

Stories ran like wildfire: there was the little girl seen on the third floor, playful, but sick, running up and down the corridor; the little boy bouncing his leather ball; a woman with bleeding wrists calling from the porch for someone to help her. Some say they saw a hearse appear, dropping off coffins at the rear of the building – this sighting many years after the sanatorium had closed down and was long abandoned.

Local kids, trespassing for a thrill, were sent terrified and screaming from Waverly Hills after invisible footsteps chased them down a corridor on the fifth floor and an angry woman's voice called from the shadows, ordering them to "Get out!"

A tunnel, which the locals call the "body chute," is central to the building's haunting. Initially built for movement of building materials during the construction of the hospital, the tunnel soon came in handy for ridding the hospital of its ever-growing number of dead. Using the body chute, a motorized rail and cable system, corpses could subtly and secretly be removed down the hill to waiting trains without patients knowing that yet another had succumbed to tuberculosis. More patients left the hospital this way, out this hidden back entrance, rather than well and walking out the front door. There are many reports of screams and an apparition of a man in a white coat beckoning for people to enter the body chute. Many believe this is the ghost of one of the orderlies given the burdensome task of loading the carriages of the body chute with the broken bodies of the dead.

The most hair-raising of the hauntings at Waverly Hills are the goings on in Room 502. Many visitors have consistently claimed to have seen the ghost of a nurse in uniform in this cold room. Consistently they have reported being told to "Get out" of Room 502.

The story goes that in 1928, the head nurse of the ward was found dead in Room 502. She was 28 and had hung herself because she was pregnant and unmarried. Depressed and desperate, she strung herself up to a light fitting. It is believed her swinging corpse was not discovered for quite some time.

This was not the only tragedy to grip Room 502. In 1932, another nurse is said to have flung herself from the window of the room. No record shows why she would have done such a thing. Many speculate she did not jump, but was pushed.

For all its gruesome past, most visitors to Waverly Hills all want to climb the stairs to see Room 502 for themselves. Call it ghoulish, but everyone, it seems, is morbidly fascinated.

Paranormal investigator and author, Troy Taylor, recalls the first time he visited Waverly Hills in 2002. He was in Louisville for the first Mid-South Paranormal Convention. The moment he saw the imposing former Sanatorium looming on the hill, he dismissed it as yet another "spooky building with a fascinating history."

He toured the building with his good friend Keith Age from the Louisville Ghost Hunter's Society. They explored every floor. Towards the end of the evening, Troy pointed out they had seen everything but the fourth floor. Keith said he had saved if for last as it was "the most active... and the most frightening."

Troy remembers clearly the moment Keith unlocked the door to the fourth floor and he got to experience it for the first time.

"I got the distinct feel that something strange was in the air," he wrote on his website Ghosts of the Prairie. "I make absolutely no claims of any psychic ability whatsoever but there was just something about this floor of the hospital that felt different to any of the others. What had been nothing more than just an old ramshackle and broken-down building suddenly seemed different.

"I can't really put into words what felt so strange about it but it almost seemed to be a tangible "presence" that I had not encountered anywhere else in the place. And right away, eerie things started to happen.

"This area was off-limits to tours and visitors. The strange thing about it was that both Keith and I clearly heard the sound of doors slamming. This was not the wind. The wind was not strong enough that night to have moved those heavy doors and this clearly sounded as though someone was closing them very hard."

As they made their way down a corridor, they approached a door that led into a treatment room. They had turned off their flashlights as they had been informed the floor was particularly "active" when no flashlights were in use.

"We made our way down the corridor using only the dim, ambient light from outside," Troy recalled. "I only noticed the doorway in the darkness because the dim light from the windows beyond it had caused it to glow slightly. This made it impossible to miss since it was straight ahead of us.

"We took a few more steps and then, without warning, the clear and distinct silhouette of a man crossed the lighted doorway, passed into the hall and then vanished into a room on the other side of the corridor!

"I got a distinct look at the figure and I know that it was a man and that he was wearing what appeared to be a long, white drape that could have been a doctor's coat. The sighting only lasted a few seconds but I knew what I had seen.

"And for some reason, it shocked and startled me so badly that I let out a yell and grabbed a hold of Keith's jacket. After my initial fright I was convinced that someone else must be on the floor with us. We turned on the lights and Keith assured me we were the only ones there but he did help me search for the intruder. There was no one else there.

"I was not the first person to have seen this mysterious figure on the fourth floor and it's unlikely that I will be the last.

"For me, this put Waverly Hills into a unique category, for there are not many places that I will firmly state are genuinely haunted. Before I can do that, I have to have my own unexplainable experience and hopefully it will be something that goes beyond a mere "bump in the night" or spooky photograph. In this case, it was much more than that because I actually saw a ghost.

"In this case, seeing really was believing. From then on I knew Waverly Hills was a lot more than just a spooky building with a fascinating history."

ABOUT THE AUTHOR

Glen Williams is a seasoned, well-respected, award winning journalist who has spent the last 30 plus years of his career working extensively in the world of magazines and newspapers. In that time he has covered world-famous stories, earning the valued trust and profiling many of the world's most treasured icons.

Along with a highly successful career in journalism, specializing in Real Life, Travel and Entertainment reporting, Glen has worked as a TV publicist and copy writer for various media organizations.

First published in 2017 by New Holland Publishers
London • Sydney • Auckland

The Chandlery, 50 Westminster Bridge Road, London SE1 7QY, United Kingdom
1/66 Gibbes Street, Chatswood, NSW 2067, Australia
5/39 Woodside Ave, Northcote, Auckland 0627, New Zealand

newhollandpublishers.com

A record of this book is held at the British Library and the National Library
of Australia.

ISBN 9781742579399

Group Managing Director: Fiona Schultz
Publisher: Monique Butterworth
Project Editor: Peter Malicki
Proof Reader: Kaitlyn Smith
Designer: Lorena Susak
Cover Designer: Andrew Quinlan
Production Director: James Mills-Hicks

Printer: Hang Tai Printing Company Limited

10 9 8 7 6 5 4 3 2 1

Keep up with New Holland Publishers on Facebook
facebook.com/NewHollandPublishers

UK £16.99
US $24.99